26
JUMPSTRAPS
Twenty Six Thumb Rules of Entrepreneurial
Bootstrapping

PRAJIT DATTA
SHANMUGAVEL SANKARAN

For Maa, Baba
&
Team Spartans
- *Prajit*

For My Wife, Two Daughters
&
FixNix Family
- *Shan*

CONTENTS

Maa and Baba - I'm not sure how to thank the people who brought me into existence. Nothing I say will ever suffice. So basically, I hope you get the gist of my life in these two words: Thank you.

Anivel Sir (my Rajnikanth), and VIT - I have so much to thank you for. Whatever I am today, is because of you and hence, for you. Under your able guidance, I have managed to flourish to the best possible of me.

And finally, a very special word of thanks for VIT Spartans. Without you, this book would have been empty. You are the reason this book is inked. Wherever I am, I will always cherish every moment spent fighting for you Spartans.

Prajit

I owe my success, my name and everything I am to my parents and my family. They have not only supported me in every aspect of my risky journey, but have also believed in me at the lowest points of it. When even I was scared to believe in myself, they did - and that's a huge thing to do.

Also, I am extremely grateful to my Nixers who have put in all their efforts to ensure that the start-up does the best it can. They've nurtured FixNix and have watched it expand. I owe them the biggest 'thank you' possible. So here it goes, a shout-out: THANK YOU Nixers!

Shan

PREFACE

Hi! Welcome to my world. I am Anamika's brain and before you venture a single word ahead, I'll be audacious enough to assume you want to get to know me a little better (After all, who doesn't?). So, here are a few points which you absolutely NEED to know about me:

1. I am cluttered as a pigsty near a chicken pen on wheels. (Wait, what?)
2. I am restless as the monkey that once snatched away the packet of biscuits right from your hand and very conveniently decided to donate it to the trash after a few seconds of rigorous pondering.
3. I am weird as *insert random Honey Singh song*
4. And most importantly, I am "busy". I love to think I work a lot, but actually end up day-dreaming for over 75% of the day (The other 25%, I spend sleeping of course).

I make life decisions under the shower. I set myself on hibernate mode in class. I design fool-proof plans of conquering the green aliens on Mars a few hours before my English term end examinations are due. I ruminate incessantly on beauty, world peace and elimination of poverty when all I'm actually supposed to do is 'illustrate the mass transfer taking place in a tannery industry'. In all, I'm just another reckless brain which finds bliss in tormenting its owner.

But hey there! Hold on! Yes, you – the brain reading this and trying to make sense of all the visual input! See, it's not like I'm trying to flirt here, but have we met before? Look! Don't get me wrong, okay? I'm just curious. Yes?

I knew it! I knew it the moment I laid my neurons on you. Actually, the point is: we brains are awesome pals (There, I just friend-zoned you so your "other half's brain won't doubt me anymore. (Don't tell me you're single. I can't help you!) Ain't I adorable? ^_^). Anyway, we conspire against our owners; we love our owners; we confound our owners; we hold our owners together (without us, I'm certain they'd be in pieces); we rebuke our owners; we provide our owners with the confidence boost (that they seldom acknowledge... But oh, well).

So now, you see brain pal, the reason I ordered Anamika's fingers to begin writing this book is that I recently figured that friends should help each other – simple! I risk sounding like Anamika's mother here but honestly, she is the kind of girl who simply loves getting... (what word do I use here)... Royally f****ed (Er... Now I have second thoughts on whether her Mom would ever dream of saying that). But honestly, she messes up her life in ways you could barely begin to imagine (It's not like I'm trying to underestimate YOUR owner, but...). Then, after she has finished creating a ruckus, she comes running back to me for help. Tell me brain pal, why do humans have this obnoxious tendency? It's so annoying! It's like, you warn them NOT to land themselves in such deep shit, you tug their hair, pull their clothes, slap them hard in the faraway hopes of waking them up from their eternal slumber of brainlessness and inevitable heart-break and YET, they go and ravage their perfect lives, cry their eyes out, wallow in self-pity and regret and BOOM! Before you know it, they've returned to you to ask for 'a solution to the problem' because apparently, 'the precaution didn't make enough sense'!

Dear fellow brains,
My neurons reach out to all of you who have ever had to deal with such hopeless owners. I understand and whole-brainedly empathize with you. This book is dedicated to you – the brains who have made it through thick and thin, the brains who haven't (hopefully) left their owners despite everything, the brains who have always believed in standing up for themselves, the brains who have been courageous enough to work alone when every other brain they ever relied upon left their side, the brains who have proved to the world that grey matter STILL exists on planet Earth, the brains who want to make it big in their lives, the brains who have ideas only THEY can conjure, the brains who carry the world forward with every thought they think. This book is dedicated to the REAL brains in a sea of dysfunctional models. This book is dedicated to the brains who have officially absorbed the fact that they can, should and must work wonders, solely because it's an obligation to their own selves and to no one else. This book is dedicated to the brains that have now successfully finished reading the first few lines of a book that may forever free those brains of all fears and spur them into action.
This book
      Is dedicated
            To
                  You, my brain pal!
Yours faithfully,
Anamika's brain

PROLOGUE

One especially jobless Friday afternoon, as I sat forlornly attempting to comprehend the meaning of life while staring at an especially obstinate question on an especially intimidating worksheet, I received a call.

So here comes disaster number 1: The phone was on the table. Anamika was on the bed. I was feeling terribly lazy. Some calculation and a lot of strenuous logic later, I figured that it was physically impossible for her to get the phone without lifting the rest of the body from the bed (even if she stretched herself to her limits). So that left me with one solution: I fervently prayed God would knock some sense into the caller and he would decide to hang up. As usual, God decided against it.

Grudgingly, Anamika tugged at the charger wire from her bed hoping she could get the phone to slide smoothly across the table to her side.
CRASH!

It seems the phone had slid too smoothly, too fast and too far.
I screamed, "REFLEX!"

Anamika jumped out of the bed and tried to make her way to the table as soon as possible.

Here goes disaster number 2: There was a packet of Lay's and a bottle of water right next to her bed, both of which were open. Very gracelessly, she stepped, tripped, somersaulted and fell over the Lay's with a melodious resounding thud on the marble floor. And just when I'd decided things couldn't get any worse, the shameless bottle of water emptied itself on her head.

By the time she had picked herself and her phone up, I was fuming. Like, literally! I could feel the blood around me bubble with that oh-so-warm-and-fuzzy emotion called "irrevocable anger".

"Anamika, can you do me a favour?" the voice on the phone asked.
"Of course, I can, you moron! I just bruised half my face and three-fourth of my limbs for you! Of course, I'm in full form to do you a 'favour'!" Anamika wanted to say.

But even though I knew perfectly well that this was legal, I warned her against it. She complied for once (thankfully!) and ended up with a polite, "Sure, tell me how I can help!"
In the moments that followed, I realised how crucial those six words had been to the compilation of this book (No, you don't have to go back and count the number of words in that sentence. Trust me when I say something, okay?) Had I not told Anamika to hold her tongue that day, perhaps today, I wouldn't be able tell you any of this either. And I'm certain she appreciates my existence a little now (She better do. I know I'm awesome)!

That one phone call led to the birth of this book. It turns out that the 'favour' the caller wanted was for her to pen down a book: on the lives of three different people, at three different stages, with three different perspectives –

at one single junction. He wanted her to pen down a book on the sealed secrets of entrepreneurship in life, redefined for ordinary brains with extra-ordinary potentials.

And just when everything seems to be picture perfect, WHOOSH! Disaster number 3 strikes. It appears that she had a time limit set for her: One month. The book had to be written, edited and published in just 30 days! I revolted. I revolted so strongly that... Well, it's unimaginable how strongly I revolted! It just didn't feel right. After all, she was an extremely naïve writer and this would be her debut. I've heard authors spend years on their first novels. I warned her. I told her this was another crazy decision. I told her she would just mess everything up all over again. Yet, this time, she didn't listen. She didn't want to listen. In fact, she coaxed me into listening to her. She lured me with her visions. She seduced me with her hopes. Till, at the end, I HAD to give in. But on one condition: I would author the book. She hesitantly agreed.

So, here I am today, filled to the brim with caffeine and memories, trying to give physical form to a seemingly crazy idea at the stroke of a Saturday midnight. So buckle up your brain-belts and get ready for three different roller-coasters in one single ride!

FLIPPING COINS

"Some people get everything they want out of life!" Rehan scowled from the sofa, with his legs spread out awkwardly in front of him, a bowl of popcorn in his hand, and his back aligned at a most abnormal angle to the arm-rest. A little about Rehan: He is the most turbulent, hyper-energetic, annoying, yet one of the best children you'll ever meet. He has a brain for keeps. And that's precisely what he does. He "keeps" it stashed away and safe, so that not much of it ever gets utilized. But that's kind of okay. After the things his cerebrum has conceived and his tongue has unleashed, I'm pretty sure that if he began using the whole of his brain, the Earth would soon have to meet a slow, painful death.

Rehan, if ever you happen to read this book, please (for GOODNESS sake) pretend as if you haven't read your introduction. And if you can't do that, please try not to condemn me to hell. (You know you need me to save your ass when Mom wonders where all the Hershey's kisses disappear from the fridge overnight. Ouch! I wasn't supposed to mention that, was I?)

Right now though, his posture clearly reminded me of a mangled up spider! This was the 10th episode of Doraemon he'd watched that day. And with every passing episode, it seemed to me that his frustration with life was increasing a hundred-fold. It stuns me as to how people can be foolish enough to do things that clearly just depress them.

"Why don't you do something, let's say like, a little more productive, Rehan? You've been tormenting the poor sofa all day long. I almost pity it now. And just for kicks, let's add that you really do resemble a couch-potato these days!"

"Can't you mind our own business?" comes the immediate reply, his eyes still glued to the television set.

I blanche, "Rehan, don't you think I deserve a little more respect than the crap you've been giving me recently?"

For a moment, Rehan takes the pains to unglue his obviously-wrecked eyeballs and quickly bless me with one glance. He manages to figure out that I'm actually seething with rage and in no mood for a worthless tongue-fight.

So he quickly handles the situation, "But don't you see? These stories have the potential to depress you as well as to make you go crazy with inspiration!"

So Rehan-ishly dramatic! Inspiration, it seems. I turn sceptic, "Oh that explains everything! Is that the reason you're dancing on cloud 99 right now, Mr. 'I-hate-my-life'?"

Rehan throws me a look which instantly makes me feel like a sinner condemned to a thousand years in Dante's inferno. I recoil in silence.

"Look, there are two ways to look at it: Nobita is the luckiest guy on the planet because he has Doraemon to solve all his problems! So technically, he seems to get everything he wants just by cribbing about it to his "friend"! But then there's a completely different perspective too. Because Doraemon gives him everything he wants, he is so dependent on this cat of his that he can't even exist a day without him! One day without this cat, and this guy literally ruins his life! So while scene A depresses me, scene B
makes me glad that at least my life doesn't revolve around a freaking CAT!"

Now, if you analyse his argument, you plainly fall head over heels in love with this weird couch-potato of mine despite accepting the fact that he can be a complete jerk whenever you turn his jerk-mode on. I know I did. You know, that's the thing about 10-year olds. No one takes them seriously. They're supposed to be nothing more than 'immature kids who haven't yet embarked on the journey of life'. But most of the time, the people who say this are extremely misled. Trust me, the best lessons my world has ever provided me, have been from those 'immature kids' - adults are pretty useless when it comes to teaching life-lessons. Try listening to the kids sometime. I'm sure they'll teach you loads of stuff with absolutely real-time examples. And you know the best part? They'll never even brag to you about having taught you anything later – because they just wouldn't know it themselves! It's a win-win situation every single time!

"So that's it?" Anamika asked me, fascinated, "Everything has two sides? You just look at the best side that makes you happy, and turn away from the bad side which makes you unhappy?"

I went into my exercise mode for a while, "No, not really. I guess you just look at one side of the coin. Then, flip it over and stare at the other side for a while just for the heck of it. Ultimately, you end up spending more time over the side which has more to convey! Whichever side tells you more, I think you would stare harder at it – and in the process, gather more information from it. So while you look at both the sides, you can read more meaning into only one side. Keep that side with you. 'Nobita cribbing to Doraemon to get things done' makes less sense. 'Nobita being dependent on Doraemon' is more telling. Both of these sentences mean the same in essence, though."

We brains are poor, deprived elements – deprived of compliments, deprived of the love of our own owners, even deprived of the things we know we deserve! So when that day, Anamika honestly praised me for my work, I knew for certain that I'd done some truly impressive job!

Thus began the quest to search for the 'meaningful' sides of all the 'coins' I've ever had.

And on the quest, I tripped across two fabulous story-tellers and entrepreneurs: People who, (unlike the lazy-bones owner I have to handle everyday), have made stuff happen in their lives; people who (instead of whining about the 'endless boredom of this lowly human world') have created stuff from scratch; people who have lived!

Thank you Rehan! For all the coins, for all the advice, for all the stories, for all the absurd logic, for everything!

[1]
APPRECIATE THE PEOPLE WHO APPRECIATE THE RISK YOU'RE TAKING

'It's just a phase,'

I remember when Anamika was in tenth grade; I had this inexplicable pull towards humanities and the liberal arts. As an avid reader, I worshipped Crossword and the British Library and no amount of bribe would pull me away from those two. In fact, the case was so bad that when a few years later, Anamika finally told Aishwarya that she had a huge crush on this guy in college, the first question she was asked was: "Oh, another one? Which book does he live in?"

But you see, if you're a student in India, you are doomed if you even DARE to think of anything beyond computer science engineering and electronics & communication engineering. The most 'logically ideal' flow of events in the life of an Indian high school graduate is:

Be born → Let your parents brag about who you look like when in reality, you look like a bag of potatoes

→ Learn to walk → Let your parents brag about how quickly who learnt something that actually comes innately to human beings

→ Attend the most expensive play-school your parents can afford → Let your parents brag about your IQ when in reality, your brain is still busy figuring out what connections to make and where

→ Learn to talk → Brag about the latest PS3 your Uncle from Sweden has gifted you

→ Attend the most expensive high school you get admitted into → Brag about how every teacher considers you her 'pet'

→ 'Crack' the X boards with any score above 99.9% → Brag about your score

→ Study 'science' → Brag about how awesome you find the subject, so others think you're a cool nerd

→ Give up on your life → Brag and call that 'dedication to doing something in life'

→ Rot in junior college during the mornings and in 10-hour long 'IITian-generating machines' in the evenings → Brag about your score in the weekly tests

→ Computer science engineering from IIT-B → Brag about your college

→ Get a job in any IT firm for "experience" → Brag about your job

→ MBA from *insert random college from the United States* → Brag about how the culture has influenced your life

→ Get a job in any MNC → Brag about the 'workplace atmosphere' whereas in reality, you'd do anything and everything to return home just an hour early
→ Toil away to oblivion → Brag about your terrific work and complain about your heartless boss
→ Marry → Brag about your trophy wife
→Have kids → Brag about them being just as smart as you
→Grow old → Realise that bragging gets you nowhere
→ Be miserable → Call it 'mid-life crisis'
→Retire → Die
Sweet and simple
Makes perfect sense too

The ONLY problem arises if the student begins to THINK for himself and doesn't allow the society to think for him. Our education system tries to ensure that there exists no student who can think for himself, but of course, every once in a while, there comes along a rotten brain like me which finds solace in slapping convention and driving a stake through societal norms. Once the student begins to make his own decisions, his life 'becomes a wreck', his parents try to 'set him back on trail', his friends try to 'make him understand', his teachers tell him 'not to divert from the purpose of his life', his girlfriend threatens to 'leave him if he can't get her a proper living'! ALL because he wants to chase his own dreams and not the dreams that the society has dreamt up for his generation!

As luck would have it, I am the sort of brain who loves to fiddle with the society. It amuses me. It has got me into a lot of trouble since childhood. But there's sheer pleasure in challenging those umpteen stupid "conventions", tattering them up on the face of the public, and letting them go to hell.

That's precisely what I did.

I swore on myself that come what may, I was not going to study CSE and follow it up with MBA.

I broke the news to my Mom a few days into standard 10. For a minute, I imagined her world would fall apart, everything she had ever done for me would have been deemed 'unsatisfactory' in her head, I would be branded as an ungrateful prodigal daughter for the rest of my life, all that she had ever taught me would have been supposed to have effectively 'gone to hell', an emotionally taxing song from an emotionally taxing Ekta Kapoor serial would begin to play in the background, the atmosphere would crumble into nothingness, her eyes would well up with those drops of glistening maternal tears and I would have to hang my head in shame for 'tainting the family name'.

The next moment, I figured that it wasn't the atmosphere, but my anticipations that had crumbled into nothingness. All my mother did was smile and pat me on my back, "I believe in you, kid!" (She has this extremely annoying habit of calling me 'kid' no matter how old I get), "You'll move mountains if you want to. Go, live life your way!"

Okay, now, this wasn't something I was expecting and even though some part of me was elated, I think I was a little disappointed too. I had expected some heavy dose of Bollywood drama. Mom gave me a simple, real-life,

9

sane reaction. Basically, I had expected a screening of Balikavadhu. But I received nothing more than a Facebook thumbs-up. Okay, I could live with that I guess.

The real tragedy struck a few months later – when Ritu Aunty found out about it.

"Oh Sumi! I'm so sorry!" she sympathised with Mom as if she had just helped her recover from a brain haemorrhage, "She used to be such an intelligent girl. Who would have thought she'd take such a stupid decision. But anyway, it's all in her fate probably. It's her destiny. Maybe this is what was written in her stars,"

Holy hell! What did I hear? Stars? Fate? Destiny? DUDE! It was my choice; it was my desire. I wanted Humanities. So I would pursue it! Simple as that! The stars were aligned just as they freaking should be!

Soon, word spread across to all the Aunties of the planet and they decided to wage war. "This cannot happen!", "She was so brilliant! What happened to the Anamika we knew?", "Aww, everything will be okay,", "God will make her understand,", "It's just a phase!", and most importantly, "Who will marry her? Today, even boys look for well-educated girls!"

I stood there aghast as all these sermons made their way into me. Well-educated? Did the liberal arts condemn you to doom? What were they talking about?

I made a mistake there. I thought too much about it. I

usually tend to over-think. And that's precisely what I did. Someone I once loved recently taught me what a mistake that was. He wrote to me: "Think, but don't over-think." But the problem with me is that I just don't know where to draw the line between thinking and over-thinking! I sometimes wish I could ask him that. But somehow, I get this weird gut-feeling that he wouldn't be able to answer me on that. I thought of the 'security issues', 'social issues', 'future issues', ' career prospects' and a dozen more useless things that shouldn't have mattered at all. I decided finally to overrule myself and 'go with the flow'.

Guys, if there's anything in my life I have ever regretted, it was that decision. To go with the flow

Because at the end of the day, only dead fish go with the flow
All this happened, as you can tell, due to all the wrong associations with all the wrong people who didn't believe in me either because they didn't know me well enough or because they did know me well enough to realise how happy I would have been had I stuck with my decision. There aren't many people around here who genuinely want you to be happy, you know.
So make sure you AVOID them to the best possible extent. Appreciate only the ones who have eyes and hearts good enough to appreciate you. If you listen to anyone else, you'll end up with tons of regret, which no one else will ever share.

*   *   *   *

'Dude! We should absolutely do it!'

Something we VITians would absolutely agree with is that there may be a trillion ways in which our FFCS (Fully Flexible Credit System) screws us over, but it also provides us with tons of new friends and acquaintances every semester (especially helpful if you are trying to avoid your ex who unfortunately happens to be in your own batch and in your own year. He doesn't essentially have to be in your own class! You can CHOOSE to opt for different slots! Had FFCS not been your saviour, then trust me, even God couldn't have saved your soul!). This turns out to be a very important asset in the long run because with new acquaintances comes new worldviews, with new worldviews comes more tolerance and with more tolerance comes better understanding (Wow! That escalated fast!). Also, every person you meet comes with an arsenal of talents and beliefs. They come with a 'frequency' of their own. And if you match the frequency of an acquaintance head on, you click, talk and have a friend for life!

So in the second semester when the students returned, Prajit discovered some totally weird people in totally weird classes with totally weird teachers teaching totally weird subjects (Bingo!). Now the thing about weird things is that however weird they are, if they are positive about their weirdness, they ROCK! (I hope I haven't lost you on my incessant banter yet because the real story begins here)

As every sane college student knows, the last few benches in any class are the epitomes of enormous talent.

You can literally dig gold in those few benches solely because they bear on themselves people with highly functional brains who do not hibernate in class, but do something much more productive – like brush up on essential life-skills like flirting (*Hats off, respect*)! Rudra happened to be one such guy. A creative mechie, Rudra was the not-so-typical engineer-in-the-making who could write poems, flirt with fervour, text, single-handedly network with the most 'important' seniors, and yet, pretend to be a truly sincere student (Yeah, remember? We all have that one 'LoL' friend!)

His contacts got him places (Seniors, you know). He not only breezed into the Riviera and Gravitas (College fests... More on them later) organization teams, but also headed the CSRD (Centre for Sustainable Research and Development) in his first year itself!

As it turns out, it all began one fated Friday afternoon when classes ended at 12 noon (Lesson learnt: Teachers take note: You should cancel afternoon classes every Friday. The mere contemplation of an extended weekend makes students so much more creative). A few of the back-benchers decided to go to Olive's kitchen for lunch (Okay, doesn't sound like a 7-star eatery. But hey! Have you heard of this word notoriously known as 'a hostel mess'?)

One random idea in one random head at one random moment got everything rolling. It was just that Rudra had suggested an online poetry writing contest for Riviera '12. Now, here's the catch: You may think that this is an easy-to-think-of, unimaginative, bland old idea. But hello! This is YOU talking. A few years down the lane when Facebook wasn't half as big as it is today, an online poetry contest was a brand new, free and innovative idea. Yes, it's the same old saying: Everything that is old and clichéd today was naïve and new yesterday.

"But dude! Do you think this will work? I mean, we're just freshers! How many people on campus actually know us? Why would they even bother to participate in a stupid online contest organised by some stupid bunch of first-years? They'll think they have better work to do for Riviera. And anyway, look at how busy everyone is! Arranging stalls, handling celebrity guest-care, getting registrations for huge events... Should we do it?" For a split second, Rudra doubted his own idea.

A moment of silence ensued.
"We should ABSOLUTELY do it! We have nothing to lose! What's at stake here?" our future-founder announced.
They had the idea, they had the spark. Now there were two things that could have happened:
- They could have laughed it off as impractical and unfeasible
- They could have been crazy enough to think this idea could actually work out

They did the latter.
They not only appreciated the idea, they decided to work for it regardless of what "others" said or thought. They didn't even bother to ask the "others". They were crazy enough to conceive the idea; they knew they could be crazy enough to execute it! After all, that's who they

were: Weird friends in weird classes eating out at weird places and getting high on weird ideas! The only weird thing is that they were even weird enough to BELIEVE this could create a ripple through the campus (if not a wave) VIT had never seen an online poetry contest before and it was bound to spark some interest.

They took the first step in faith and appreciation of each other. The rest is on office record as 'the first online event on campus'.

*   *   *   *

"It's simple! I didn't!"

I remember when I first met the Chief Nixer of FixNix, Inc., after a 4 hour long chat over coffee and ice-cream, the final question I asked (and the one I'd been dying to ask all the time) was: Sir, how did you know your idea would work?

Shan Sir smiled, "It's simple! I didn't!"
I was left baffled for a while, "Didn't your parents and friends always support you and tell you it would?"

I thought people who took risks always had tons of people supporting them and cheering for them all the while. After all, when others believe in you, your faith in your abilities increases immensely.

"The question isn't about all the others believing in you, Anamika. It's about who you associate with! I choose to surround myself with positive people. I choose to stick to

15

the decisions I make. I choose to be happy. I choose everything!"

Suddenly, I found myself drifting away to something I'd read in the cell biology and genetics class (Of course, remember, I warned you I'm messed up! I drift off to completely insane topics at completely insane times. Not my fault you chose to keep reading!) So, there happens to be this thing called apoptosis in cells: it's a mechanism of cell death. There was this point in one of the slides of the PowerPoint presentation: "Most cells die if they fail to receive some specific survival signals from the other cells." I think this sentence suddenly struck a corner – struck hard! And it's absolutely true, you know? Trust me, I'm a brain. I have first-hand experience of how neurons begin to behave the moment their surrounding neurons begin to become unfriendly towards them – they wither from within... and then they die.

Isn't this fascinating? My 'human' neurons aren't very different from simple algal blooms when it comes to survival. We absolutely ought to surround ourselves with positive 'survival factors'. The negatives will kill us.
This is a big thing to acknowledge. It seems CEOs do!

[2]
BEND THE RULES

'I guess we always do'

"Hey, Anamika, I was just wondering if you could... You know, umm... Like, just saying, but do you think you could... Come out for a coffee someday... With me?" he finished on an extremely awkward note, his hands fixed in his pockets and his eyes fixed to his shoes.

Finally! It had taken him seven months to finally ask her out. I'd been waiting for this since the day we'd met. Finally the wait seemed to be worth it.

But I'll let you in on a secret here: Classic coffee dates have never really appealed to me. Well, to play it safe, of course that is the best possible first timer. But let's cut the cheese guys! It's so boring! What do you even do? You waltz up to some expensive 'classy' cafeteria in some expensive 'classy' section of some expensive 'classy' mall, spend a few hundred bucks on something as ubiquitous as coffee, stare at the ceiling, stare at the television behind the glass walls, stare emptily at your hands and feet, weirdly stare into each other's eyes and try to figure out what he is thinking (Mind it, no romantic orchestra strikes up though), while he's thinking EXACTLY the same things as you are:

1. Oh my God! I hope I don't screw this up!
2. How do I look?
3. Dear Cupid, please don't let me look like I looked when I woke up this morning!
4. What the heck is going on in his head?
5. Am I fidgeting too much?
6. Am I making enough sense? Or do I appear to be a weirdo?
7. It's me who's doing all the talking! Do I come off as too desperate?

DUH! Snap out people! We ALL know how that works. In fact, honestly, I can't even remember the number of so-called 'dates' I've spent thinking the ditto same things over and over again and wondering what the tagline ("A lot can happen over coffee.") actually meant.

I'm currently in that phase of life in which if you take me out to CCD once more, I'll just smile sweetly at you, perhaps blush a little, take out a gun and shoot you pointe blanc on the head. (Yeah, stop complimenting me; I know I'm adorable!)

Yes sweetheart, I hate to break it to you but it is high time you break out your bubble. The cafeteria was just trying to sell itself with that tagline. Nothing (absolutely NOTHING!) happens over coffee if you don't make it!

Yet, this was the only guy who did things differently – ever! Just as everything was getting (as usual) very monotonous (what do you like doing, what are your hobbies, where have you lived, blah, blah, blah...), he almost screamed in the middle of the lounge, "DUDE! Is this what you're supposed to do on your first date?!"

"Yeah, right?" I quipped in

"This is so boring! I need some zing! How much more time do we have?"

I glanced at the watch. It was 11 am. The guy seemed to have something up his sleeve, "We have all day!"

We turned that classic old-fashioned date into a wild, out-of-the-world God-forsaken adventure! From bungee jumping to racing up flyovers at 120 kmph at midnight, from breaking into a movie theatre without tickets to running out of fire exits, we did everything we shouldn't have done on a first date! I ended up with a fabulous partner in crime that day – someone I'll always treasure, however far he goes.

Later that week, Aishwarya asked me, "But that… that's against the rules!"

"It is!"

"Rule #1 of the Rule-book says 'Thou shalt sit down at the coffee table and get to know each other.'"

"But you get to know so much more about each other when you're trying to escape a theatre from the fire exits! You know just how much of an adrenaline rush they get and how they handle overly stimulating situations. You'd never be able to make that out by just asking them, would you?"

Aishwarya nodded in bewilderment.

"So you broke the rules and discovered something better?!"

"I'm not particularly sure, but I guess we always do…"

*　　　　*　　　　*　　　　*

'This was just one of the rules we bent!'
"But what about the DSW? Didn't they object?"
Prajit threw his head back and laughed as Anamika sat there baffled, "Well brain, what's so funny here?"
"Wait, moron! There has to be a sane reaction to this," I replied.
"Yes, I think they would have… if they had known!"
That's great! So all this was being done undercover? For a moment, I flared, "But how's that legal?"
The Department of Student Welfare (DSW) is this wing of authority which keeps a check on every activity conducted by the students and for the students. I don't think I'm supposed to tell you this (but I'll tell you anyway, as I usually do) but the students' fondly refer to it as the 'Hawk' of the university. Nothing escapes its eyes and it's always on the prowl. It has been rumoured that somewhere in the dark dungeons of the DSW, there are columns and columns and more columns of endless files and folders of records of events and invites and also student-prisoners, who once tried to do stuff without 'the prior notice of the DSW'. It was nothing less than a criminal offence!

"No, it's not legal, but we were kids! We didn't know there existed something called the DSW!"

"Oh!" that sort of warmed me up to the criminal confession.

"We printed 100 copies of the poster and dispatched them off to be stuck all over campus with absolutely no knowledge of what paperwork was to be done and what permissions would be required. And after 5 days of efficient publicity, the event was all set for take-off! And we were amazed to see that everything had actually borne fruits! 15 minutes prior to commencement, we already had 16 posts on our Facebook page: VIT Spartans."

"Pause, pause, pause!" I butted in, "Let's get back to the major issue: How the heck did you manage to avoid the DSW?"

Prajit laughed, "You can't really call that 'avoid', can you?"

"I'm still waiting for the excuse,"

"I'm afraid the excuse is not very convincing. You see, all this started because of a random idea on a random lunch table and we were random freshmen! How much do you think we knew about VIT? We genuinely didn't know there existed some part of the University called the DSW, let alone the fact that it needs 'prior notice'!"
"That's just sad…"

"No, you know what, it isn't! In fact, I'd rather take it as a blessing, though it did get us into some soup later,"

"Oh, do you usually consider everything that goes wrong a 'blessing'? Or is this situation unique?" I was beginning to get jealous of his optimism!

"No, not very unique. The point is that if we knew that there was a hell lot of paperwork and running around after authorities involved, we'd have been too scared to DO anything at all! We'd have procrastinated (to oblivion), or in better words, never had the balls to do anything beyond thinking and planning! Often to get what you want, you need to bend the rules – not break them, but at least bend them. This was just one of the rules we bent unintentionally!"

*   *   *   *

'It's what we Indians call jugaad!'

"How many?"
"Innumerable,"
I laugh hard, "So you're trying to tell me that you've been just as bad as my brother when it comes to stealing stuff? In this case, advice?"
"Precisely,"
"But why do you do that? You could have thought for yourself, couldn't you?"
"Expert advice never hurts, nonetheless,"

I could do nothing but agree to this, "But why sneak into start-up conferences? You could have easily attended them as a member, right?"
"College teaches you a lot of things, Anamika. What it doesn't teach you is that sometimes, you MUST bend the rules. And bend it often. Bend the rules when you don't have the required resources. It's technically like beg, borrow, or steal! But if you want something really bad, you've got to have it!"

"So what you're selling is…"

"That ends justify the means. Yes, absolutely!"
"You didn't have the required resources to attend as a

22

member?"

"No, there came a time when we were walking a financial tight-rope. Yet, I made sure I snuck into every single conference I found. Another important thing to note here is that contacts can get you places. If you are lucky enough to personally know the coordinators of the conference, make use of it! It's what we Indians call 'jugaad'. You have the resources, you have the contacts, exploit them to their limits!"

[3]
CHASE THE PEOPLE WHO MATTER

Living for you

The other day I was whining to this epic guy over phone about this woeful and nomadic life of mine when we stumbled across the debatable topic of 'memories'.

"Life sucks... and then you die!" I stated with oomph, quoting a quote I'd read somewhere long ago and which made perfect sense at that particular stage of life.

"But on the way, you make memories,"
"Yeah, woeful memories, full of moistened eyes and downturned smiles,"
"Hey, you're being a jerk, you know sweetheart!"

"Absolutely, and you're being a useless consoler, you know... onion-heart?" I said the word at then cringed at how unimaginative I was getting by the day.

"Look, you make memories... and then you die!"

"How do you choose who to make memories with? Point your expectations at one person and he breaks both - you as well as your expectations! No one is worth making memories with. No one is worth dying for."

"The delegate of the Angels would like to raise a point of order to what Ms. Depressed-and-Hopeless has just said,"
"Ha! The delegate of the Angels, eh? Look at how self-obsessed you can get!"
"May I have your permission instead of having you brood over my impeccable word-art which clearly never fails to enthral you?"
"Cut the crap and go on!" I give in.

"There exists a flaw in the last assertion you just made, Ms Depressed-and-Hopeless: There are many people worth dying for, because that is only logically consistent. In the long run, we're all dead anyway. So how does it even matter who you DIE for? It's inevitable. We might as well do it for any random person we meet if he needs it. What matters is who we LIVE for. If you ask me if I'll die for you, my answer would obviously be a big, fat yes! But will I live for you? I would have to mull that question over in my head. The day I begin to live for you is the day you'll finally have won me over,"

For a moment, I got dizzy, "And... who will you live for, Shrey?"
"Only for someone who matters,"

*   *   *   *

'Chuck the ones that don't!'

Just before GraVITas '12, as they were trying hard to zero in on some appropriate events, a question struck the team.

"Aniket came up with the idea of sponsorships. The last time we'd held an event, we had had to shell out some cash from our own pockets (and sadly enough, it wasn't even 'some'. It was a HELL lot) for the prize distribution. It would be so much more... let's say, 'economical', if someone else did the paying for us this time," Prajit tells me. I nod vigorously. I've handled the pains of cash-less-ness long enough. In the first semester, I'd been given the liberty to 'budget my own expenses' and as was expected of me, I'd screwed up majorly.

What they did next was (according to Prajit) the most stupid thing they could have done (though I'm pretty sure I'd have done the same. And hey, you stop judging us okay? You'd have done the same too!)

This is what followed:
"Perhaps we could ask a GraVITas '12 sponsor to help us out with our events too,"
"No, not just the pre-existent ones – let's try to reel in some other companies too. I bet anyone will be willing to advertise on such a diverse campus!"
"Yes, let's get hold of some institutions which are swimming in ready money and make it huge!"

*   *   *   *

"No one cared about the events anymore; all we could gush about was whether to get Bill and Melinda Gates to sponsor us, or whether we could 'settle for' a more desi variant like Tata. In the heat of the moment, we built not only built castles in the air, but also decided the minute details: like what colour the exteriors should be painted with, what sort of beds the bedrooms should have, whether we would put up Michelangelo or Da Vinci near the stairs and even what biscuits would be served with the English tea every morning!" Prajit laughs.

"Well, people get caught up all the time. But why was that such a stupid thing to do?"

"Because it shifted our focus away from the priorities! The end result was that we drafted mails to our 'prospective sponsors' without the necessary event details, because holy hell! We ourselves hadn't had the time to decide the event details! Tell me the name of one corporate ignoramus who would be willing to sponsor an event about which he didn't know shit!"
I sympathized, "Poor you!"

"Yeah, poor us!" he agreed, "But hey, that taught us something too, didn't it? We needed to set our priorities right: Reach out for the things that truly count and chuck the ones that don't! Sponsors hardly matter when participants are nil."

*   *   *   *

'Customers matter, not investors!'

"So, you're trying to say that in the whole process of setting up FixNix, you didn't approach investors at all?" I asked, genuinely mortified.
"I never had to!"

"What the heck?" I asked Anamika, even more mortified.

"Look, it is pretty simple: You have a product. You think the product is useful. You approach customers. You sell it. They pay you. Investors automatically drop out of nowhere! When I started FixNix, I did it entirely with my own personal investments. But then, I went and put my product and ideas out there for the public to see and judge. Customers draw investors. No one will be willing to invest in a product that doesn't sell!"

"Yeah, but I've always thought that investors were egoistic morons who wouldn't come uninvited," I state matter-of-factly.

Shan Sir looks amused, "Of course they are! But then, it's not just words which invite every time, Anamika. Sometimes, it's actions. Let's face it now. No one in this era does anything without some personal (very often ulterior) motive attached to it,"

I cringe. I hate it when things like these are slapped right onto me. Okay, I know, I know people are mean and selfish, but knowing is different from accepting. I still find it hard to believe when people break my faith in them and tell me I'd been wrong to 'expect too much' from them. Bloody hell! I expected because I unfortunately thought you had the potential to live up to my expectations. Naina has tried at least a zillion times to drive some sense into me and yet, no amount of drilling helps. I still feel vulnerable. I still cry like a blubbering baby when something or someone I prioritize puts me second. I know, but it still hurts all the same.

"And with investors, well, you know very well what they want – a heavy bank balance. They want their investments to bear them fruits and it's absolutely natural they would. Till date I haven't come across a single investor who gets lured by words and an empty chequebook. There aren't many 'Mother Teresa's who have walked the planet of the entrepreneurs either, who are willing to donate generously and expect nothing in return." He continues, "I remember giving a guest-talk at a conference once, wherein I was asked to present the cyber-security solutions we had proposed. After the conference, I was approached by a few prospective customers. After I'd successfully sold my idea to them, another group of people flocked in out of nowhere. I turned to them expecting them to be another new bunch of customers. But all they said was, 'Sir, we are impressed by your proposal. We saw the previous customer group you entertained. If you could give us a solid plan, we're willing to invest. This idea can generate a ripple in the market'. I stood at the podium, unsure how to react. I'd just given them a piece of my idea and here they were telling me they were willing to help me shape it!"

I 'wow' in wonder, "So you don't have to approach

investors at all! That sounds like a dream for any entrepreneur!"

"Nah, not really. It takes WAY bigger dreaming to even hit the track of entrepreneurship," he winks slyly.

[4]
DON'T LOITER

User is offline.

You don't necessarily have to CREATE new problems in order to solve them. The world has seen an undesired excess of problem creators anyway. (So, leave that to the terrorists – unless, you are a terrorist. If so, then go, create more problems. All the best!)

The problem arises when we human brains begin suicide bombing for no reason – just because we're in a mood to kill ourselves. We have this epic weapon of complete destruction to (you guessed it right) "over-think"! We absolutely love to torture our owners with every signal we fire. (Tell me brain pal, be honest, your owner doesn't have to know. Just a secret between you and me - Don't you do the same?)

Let me give you an example you'll relate to.

Suppose there's this person you (sort of) have the hots for. And one fine day, you receive a text from him. You are elated; you're on the seventh heaven. You're dancing around in glee, when all of a sudden, you're reminded that you have to text back.

"Okay, so he said 'hi!' with an exclamation mark at the end. That's a good sign, isn't it? It means he's thinking about me and wants to talk to me! Oh my God! Am I dreaming?"

"Umm... But wait! Why didn't he send me a smiley with the 'hi!'?"

"Okay, this is ridiculous! Maybe he doesn't really want to talk to me. He just has some work. How many classes do we have in common? Well, plenty! Maybe he just wants to ask me the homework in the Multivariable Math class,"

"Bingo! That's it! Guys are all the same! They are all jerks! They are all creeps! They would never ever text you first to ask how you were doing or what you've been up to recently! All they'll do is text when they have some work! What am I? His secretary? His personal assistant? It's always either work or something he needs. And you know Anamika? All guys 'need' just one thing. If so, they can just call you up one night and tell you they are thinking of you! But no, they'll do something entirely different. They'll text you in the day to make you feel special. They'll create an emotional bond with you. They'll lead you on. They'll pretend to understand you. And then, at the end, when you realise it was all fake, they'll leave you broken and in pieces. He can go to hell. I'm not replying!"

3 minutes later:

"But well, are all guys the same? What if he'd texted to talk and not just for some work? What if he is a genuinely nice fellow? Perhaps, I should get back to him. I have nothing to lose here, do I? It's just an innocent 'hi!'"

5 minutes later:

Reply: "Hey! ☺"

And bam! *User is offline*

There goes your first 'hi!' – exactly where it was supposed to be: in the drain!

*　　　　　*　　　　　*　　　　　*

When you think too hard about something, it's just that you stop thinking rationally!

"Uh-oh! Now what?" Prajit's friends were honestly confused as they stared solemnly at the laptop. 'War of the Rhymes' had become a show-stopper on social media. Entries had flowed in like… like fish in the Bay of Bengal… (Phew! I can't believe I'm out of similes already). And well, it was deemed to be a 'success'. But the success had been a little too huge. Now, the question was: How were they supposed to judge amongst so many entries?

"Dude! Someone go get Hemingway back from Necropolis, please,"

"Well, the page has been trending quite high recently," someone threw in a consolation

"Hell! That's the problem! Now, the page likes have

been increasing at over 150 per day! We are doomed if we don't make appropriate judgements!"

After a dozen futile attempts at coming up with the winners, they finally gave up.

*   *   *   *

I nudged Anamika, "Why does it seem like the list of problems is never-ending? I'd have given up long back, you know!"

Anamika seared, "That's because you are a useless bag of nerves! You need guts to be this brave and keep going! Just you wait, I'll get to you soon enough!"

I decided to remain silent in the hopes that 'this too would pass.'

*   *   *   *

"That's it! We need a Round 2!"

Everyone looked at each other confounded, "Hey! Here we can't even judge these pieces of 'pretty poetry' that we have in front of our eyes right now and you want to hold a round 2? How much of excess blood do you have flowing in your veins?"

"Hey, look at it this way: Now, we can't really choose the owners because there are tons of entries. But we can at least narrow down this list, right? We can pick out the top 20, head them for another round and then, ultimately get the School of Social sciences and Language to judge! Lesser work, better results,"

This was weird. I interrupted, "So why did you need a Round 2 for that? You could very well have taken all the poems and asked the SSL to judge from the first round itself!"

"Nah, these higher authorities apparently need to be notified beforehand if you want them to help you out with something. In other words, they need appointments. And we hadn't informed them about Round 1. So, they wouldn't judge that. All we could do then is: Get their permission for round 2 and then ask them to judge it,"

An hour-long debate and a pros-and-cons chart later, the verdict was announced: "Let there be Round 2!" The idea was to give the top 20 contestants from Round 1 a comic beginning to a story and ask them to end it on a tragic note, or vice versa.

This worked out as smooth as those frictionless pulleys in HC Verma! Absolutely zero friction! Three teachers consented to judge the stories in Round 2 and finally, they had three winners.

"How did you come up with the solution? And more importantly, how did you decide to act on it? I would have lingered on the thought for too long, cooked up a 100 different reasons it wouldn't have worked and you know, when you think too hard about something, everything seems unfeasible!" I asked, awed.

"That's not true! When you think too hard about something, it's just that you stop thinking rationally! You may think you're thinking too hard, but actually, you're just kidding yourself into thinking that you're thinking! Have you ever thought too much before having a milkshake? If you do, you'll notice that there are several reasons not to have it. For example,

1. It may be stale
2. It may be doped
3. It may lead to food poisoning
4. You might end up in an ICU
5. The doctors of the hospital you end up in may try to murder you because of your past sins
6. There might be a zombie attack on the hospital at midnight and you may not be able to run because you'll have tubes of saline sticking out of your wrists!

DUH! Would you listen to all that? The best thing to do in our case is to quickly list the pros and cons of a proposed solution and advocate a quick debate. You'll have your answer in minutes! Lingering on something for some time is okay; loitering aimlessly is not!"

*   *   *   *

'Keep your filthy thoughts to yourself'

"I'd give up on all my dreams if I thought too hard," I sighed.
"No, you'd give up on all your dreams if you didn't have the courage to chase them. In other words, if you didn't have the balls,"
I revved up for a clash, "You're telling me I'm gut-less?"
(That's just an expression though. Your courage doesn't

stem from your guts, but from your brains. Trust me, I know!)

"No, Anamika!" Shan Sir laughs, "I'm just saying average human guts are not enough! And moreover, you'd have to be able to think straight. Do you know the story of the two friends who fought over thoughts?"

I shrugged and turned to a new page in my note-pad, ready to jot down whatever came next. Somewhere, a cappuccino was getting cold, but it hardly mattered.

He began, "There were two friends: one rich and one poor. Mere 'friendship' was an underestimation of the bond they shared. They had been the best of buddies since the day they had met. Once there appeared a few guests at the poor friend's door. After a lunch and a nap, he decided that the guests should see the place around. Now the problem was that the poor man didn't own a car. But he knew that his rich friend owned three. So, without even giving it a single thought, the poor friend set out to the rich friend's house.

On the way, he had an internal monologue:

'What if he doesn't want to give me the car?'

He paused for a while and hesitated mid-way, 'Oh! I'm just being negative! He's my friend after all. Of course, he wouldn't mind giving me the car!'

A while later he paused again, 'What if he refuses to lend me the car?'

'Oh God! What am I even thinking?'

He continued on his way, 'What if he insults me in public?'

'I'm sure the devil is playing around with my head!'

Finally, when he reached his rich friend's place, he rang the doorbell and immediately fell into an unending trail of terrifying thoughts. The moment his friend opened the door, the poor friend began hurling abuses at him: I know you won't give me the car! I don't even know why I'm here in the first place! I know you think I beg of things from you, but let me tell you this: I'm not here to beg, okay? Keep your filthy thoughts to yourself. Goodbye! And never talk to me again!

The rich friend was left startled and helpless and clueless as he watched his friend walk away!"

I didn't know how to respond to this.

"So you see, Anamika, it's all in your head. Everything you see, you never actually see. You perceive. Everything you perceive has to do with the current health status of your brain. So when you think too much, you begin to tumble off-track onto the wrong lines! And there, along with your mind, go your 'guts'!"

I received a sound mental thrashing from Anamika that day.

[5]
ERADICATE STUPID PREJUDICES

'You must be another heart-broken IITian then?'

June 13, 2014, Friday:

"Mid-summer Kolkata is horrendously humid," I mumble as I leave for the publishing house where I have an appointment. Dad waits for me in the car. It is my idea to keep him waiting in the A/C, so that in case I get boiled, at least he stays healthy enough to drive me home. I am currently working on a major writing project and I decide to meet a publisher to see if she can provide me with some useful tips. Since the day I first put ink to paper, I've always wanted to visit a publishing agency. So today is like a dream come true. The way I walk reminds me of the clichéd "spring in the stride" and I smile as I think of it.

"So, you write?" a middle-aged man pops out of nowhere, as I wait in the lounge.

I nod enthusiastically.
"But you look kind of young! You look like you study in college!"
"That's perhaps because I do!"

"Oh, I see! You must be another heartbroken IITian then?"
"Excuse me! I'm not an IITian and I have a non-existent love life!"
"Eh? Then what do you write about?"

*   *   *   *

That day I realised the true definition of 'Mind-blown'. The stereotype had literally 'blown away' my mind. It drained me of the energy I had entered with. It drained my stride of its spring. In fact, it also drained my heart of my love of publishing houses a little bit. I was so proud of myself for maintaining composure and not banging the man with the nearest chair that I treated myself to some well-deserved chocolate ice-cream at the first possible opportunity afterwards.

Have you ever wondered how many times we come across such stereotypes in a single day? I'll bet you can't enumerate. We're surrounded with stereotypes and prejudices in every sphere of life, right from academia ("Asians are fabulous at math,") to cuisines ("Bengalis can't tolerate spice,"), from professions ("Gujaratis are only into business,") to commenting on intelligence levels ("Blondes are stupid!") And do you know the worst part of it all? We KNOW these are stereotypes; we KNOW that these ought to be broken; we KNOW that they are harmful to the society; and yet, we choose to keep our mouths and minds shut and follow them thoughtlessly.

It's time to wake up folks! Wake up to the injustices of such baseless prejudices, wake up to the world; wake up to observe and not to judge. Wake up! It's high time we stop calling ourselves the most evolved species of the planet and finally start behaving like it! Our brains are not as limited as we make them appear. Our brains are capable of seeing every person for their own unique qualities. Our brains are meant to be left free to explore, converse, find and then judge, if at all judging is essential.

This is one incident that influenced me way more than perhaps necessary. After all, human absurdity rarely fails to impress!

*   *   *   *

'Then think better'

"I don't think any novice is Einstein-ish enough to design a poster in one hour, you know?" Prajit wasn't feeling especially hopeful that night. There's a difference between dreaming of the impossible and giving it physical form. Fine, admittedly, the idea that Rudra had come up with was brilliant. But that didn't mean it could

work overnight!
"Then think better," came the reply.

Rehaan, a hard-core, center-focused, die-hard techie, was up for the challenge. At 9 pm one random Friday night, he was bold enough to decide he could learn Photoshop within a few hours and create a poster for the publicity of this online event. Prajit looked at him with those dreamy eyes which suggest, "I wish you were right, but I know you are wrong!" But then, there was no harm in giving it a shot, right? They had nothing to lose (nothing much to gain from failure either, but that doesn't have to be mentioned). So, it was agreed that Rehaan should try it out once. Barring the disappointment, there was nothing that a failure could bring.

Two hours and 15 YouTube videos later, there was a knock on the door. Prajit braced up for the worst. Photoshop wasn't that easy after all.

"Dude, have you decided a fancy name for the event yet?" Rehaan's eyes were alight with child-like glee.
"WHAT! The poster's ready already?"
Rehaan nodded, "Ready already!"
"Are you kidding me?" this guy had had zero knowledge about a couple of hours ago. And now, here he was with a fully-designed happy poster, and an equally fully-designed happy face!
"No, I'm kidding those Photoshop guys who pretend like it takes ages to develop a picture," he smirked, "Now, name please?"
"Send Your Poems?"
"Nah, too mainstream,"

"War of the Poets?"

"Err… The people participating aren't exactly going to be 'poets', are they? Because if they are, I'm out of this place!"

Prajit laughed, "Perhaps not - Just a bunch of enthusiastic 'budding-poets' maybe?"

"Then think of something more relevant, na?"

"War of the Rhymes?"

"War of the Rhymes."

"That's pretty good, isn't it?"

"We're up dude! What are you waiting for? Your event is on AIR!"

*   *   *   *

"How did it feel back then?" Anamika asked, almost flushed with happiness herself!

"Of course it felt amazing, but more importantly, it reminded me to flush off all the stupid assumptions we hold in the back of our brains! If you THINK someone can't do something, if you assume before you begin, if you are narrow-minded enough not to let them try to prove themselves, then nothing in the whole of this universe is possible. But if you break free from those 110 useless prejudices and assumptions, you have everything at your feet! I'll always remember the lesson Rehaan taught me that day - to break free from the stereotypes of failure, to challenge the odds and to prove your capabilities, whatsoever"

*   *   *   *

'Spare your tongue the trauma'
"What is the worst prejudice you have ever come across?" I ask curiously.
"Oh prejudice! Plenty of them!"
"Tell me one."
"Yeah, well, I'll tell you the worst and the most important one: People born in villages think like villagers,"
Anamika bites her lip, "Shit! Someone actually told you that?"
"Yes, straight off!"
"And you still didn't bite off their head?"
"That would be too conventional, Anamika! Come on! I didn't expect that from you!"

I laugh, half-annoyed, half-impressed, "So what did you do?"
"Nothing said – just lent them a deaf ear. You shouldn't really argue with fools because
    A. They'll never understand
    B. You'll waste your time
    C. You'll pick a fight
    D. You'll fall to their level
    E. It's extremely demeaning to your brain,"
"So does that mean you let them talk all the while, without reacting the slightest bit?" I wonder, aloud, unsure if that was the best thing to do.
"No, obviously not!"

I sit all muddled up, "But that's what you just said!"
"No, I said you shouldn't ARGUE with fools. I never said you shouldn't SHOW them your worth. Let your actions do the talking. Spare your tongue the trauma!"

[6]
FAMILY FIRST

'This isn't working anymore!'

Remember this: Your family loves you the most in the world (unless you are Cinderella. In that case, ask your fairy Godmother for help). And the people who love you the most are usually brutally honest to you too. So, however harsh it sounds, when your parents tell you that it would be a sane decision not to rear sheep for a living, you'd better try listening to them. They most probably have a reason for it. Perhaps, it would be better for you, for your family, for the sheep, for the farm, and for the world in general.

Remember those golden days back in standard 6th when everyone around you wanted to be Hannah Montana? Well, however embarrassing it might sound, I wanted to be Hannah Montana too! (Oh come on! Don't pretend! Who didn't? Back in those days, Miss Cyrus used to be cute, okay?)

So, anyway, I got all pumped up about singing and becoming a rock-star and going on a world tour and getting famous and the list goes on. I even got myself a 'funky' (read 'disastrously sick') purple hairdo, bought a ton of other jewellery like nose-rings and anklets and bracelets and what-nots (which are now safely tucked away into some dusty wardrobe of embarrassing past memories).

Also, I began to practice on my 'vocals'.

But as luck would have it, I discovered that not everyone is blessed with a tolerable voice adapted to concert singing. Here's the catch: I discovered it. But I didn't accept it. (Yeah, yeah, I have 'acceptance issues'. After all, hearts don't give up, do they? I kept 'practicing' and tormenting everyone around me. There came a time when my friends deserted me. There came a time when my neighbours would politely smile a painfully fake smile and shut all their windows whenever I embarked on my 'practice sessions'. There came a time when everyone lost faith in my musical abilities – all but me. I kept torturing the souls who cared. I kept driving them insane. Until one fine day, my family decided to hold a round-table conference with me (at the centre of the table).

One fated Friday night, under the sinister influence of the dim lights and some delectable lasagne, my parents confronted me with a heavy heart:
"Anamika, my child, I have something to say," Dad began.

"Before you assume anything, let me tell you that this, in

no way, determines your worth as a person," Mom broke him off.

"Or, your capabilities as a person!" Dad chimed in.
"We need you to know that we love you, whatsoever and would support you in everything you wish to achieve!"
"You're a brilliant blessed child and we can't even begin to tell you how happy we are to have you as our daughter,"
Okay, will these people ever get to the point? In my greatest depths, I knew where this was leading to, but I asked Anamika to remain silent. After the gazillion disclaimers and apologies-in-advance, they were almost making me feel like a full-fed goat right before it is slaughtered. And in case you didn't know, that's not a very nice feeling.

"Anamika… We know how much you love music,"
"And, how much effort you've put into this,"
"But…"
A moment of thunderous silence followed.
"This just isn't working anymore!" they said together.
Wait a second! Why did this feel so much like a break-up talk even before I'd laid my hands on a single guy?
"I'm afraid you have to give up, Anamika. You can't keep hurting yourself and the people who love you anymore! You have to find something that loves you back as much as you love it!"
Bummer! My parents were good at this!

They sighed as they waited for my fountain of tears to erupt. But I think I knew better. I took a deep breath, blew away the music notes, brushed myself back up and smiled, "Mom, no offence, but how many guys have you broken up with before you met Dad?"

Dad burst out laughing; Mom looked shocked for a while, appeared thoughtful and answered gravely, "Just a dozen or so, I should think,"

And that, folks, is the story of how I broke up with my Hannah Montana dreams!

*   *   *   *

'They couldn't care less'

"Okay, so you didn't tell the DSW about your motives, but did you at least tell your parents what you were trying to do here on campus?" I ask, trying to make peace with the fact that Prajit had gotten so lucky in ignorance.

"Look, stop hitting where it hurts, okay?" Prajit gives me a fake 'hurt' look.

"You can't even act properly," I laugh.

"You don't say," he agrees.

"So, did your family know?" I prod, getting back to the question.

"Yes, they knew I was trying to set something up here, but they couldn't care less,"

"They didn't CARE?"

"Yeah, and it was perfectly legit you see. I have that sort of an impression back home. Nobody cares! I told them that I had a plan brewing in my head. So my Dad just told me that he knew. I've ALWAYS had plans brewing in my head. There wasn't anything new about it! And honestly, I never knew it would be successful in the first place. I mean, come on! Are you kidding me? One idea and one poster overnight don't make me the founder of a whole new club in a day, do they?"

"No, they don't,"
Prajit laughs, "When I try to be modest, it's not very polite of you to agree, okay?"
"Okay,"
"You're agreeing again!"
"Yes, I am,"
"Okay, stop being a pain. But do you get the answer to your question?"
"Yes, I do. But I wonder if that's the case with real-life corporate start-ups. They're big deals, aren't they?"
"You mean setting up a club in the first year isn't a big deal?" Prajit is almost in a mood to kill me today.
"No, no, that's not what I meant," I try to make up for the mess, but fall short of words.
"Yes, that's precisely what you meant, and no, I'm not angry as yet (though I think you're strumming at the wrong strings today), and yes, corporate start-ups are big deals... I do not think the 'family-doesn't-care' rule works out there,"

*   .   *   *   *

'Family' and 'blood relatives'

I automatically turn to face Shan Sir.
"Yeah, I'm honoured that you finally acknowledged my presence," he feigns annoyance, "I was feeling a little

49

left-out a while ago,"

"Oh, I'm so sorry! I really did not mean for this to happen,"

Shan Sir laughs, "Why aren't you in Bollywood, Anamika?" For a while I think he actually means it and I blush red, but then he continues, "You could be Ekta Kapoor's favourite over-dramatic saans or bahu,"

Prajit sneers shamelessly, while I boil, "Okay, go on, you people seem to have no better hobby than to pester me. So be it. Keep pestering..."

"Are you angry with us, Anamika?" Prajit quips in.

"Oh no, I'm ecstatic I've got friends like you to tolerate. What more could I have asked for in Heaven? You know you're going straight to Hell after this,"

"And I'm dragging you along,"

"Rest it, people, let's get back to business," Shan Sir saves the day, "So you were asking,"

"Yeah, I was asking if, while starting something SIGNIFICANT," I glance sideways at Prajit to make sure that the word sinks into his head. It doesn't, so I continue, "do you always need your family's consent?"

"No, you do not really need their consent in the beginning, because they may over-analyse and pull you back. But when you're selling something for the first time in the market, it's best to test the waters with them. They'll give you honest and unbiased feedback for your own good. Not everyone around can do that,"

I agree, "So you try out everything with your family before you make it public?"

Shan Sir laughs, "That's the way it should be. But, I work as a Chief Information Security Officer, you see. That's not something you can try at home!"
"That's a problem then,"

"Not really. When I say 'family', it doesn't necessarily mean my blood relatives. It means people who I can trust with anything. In my case, this extends to the people who work for me. I trust them a hell lot - for both positive as well as negative feedback. Whatever service we choose to air to the public, we try in the office first to test how well it works. Of course, once it is released to the public, we may stumble across new problems due to extended outreach, but at least the core problems can be eliminated in the office itself,"

[7]
AVOID GOSSIP

'By the way, who the hell are you talking about?'

It's like plague (Only, a tad bit worse).
Every school has a gossip hall which feeds on gossip-leeches. Obviously, mine was no exception. The biggest problem was that these gossip-leeches mostly belonged to the 'kewl kids' group. You understand the meaning of this 'kewl kids' group, don't you? These were the people who were deemed to exist at the zenith of popularity. Whatever they did would be aped diligently by the rest of the school. They set the trends: right from pink highlights on brunette hair to tattered denims, right from Lady Gaga style blue eyeliners to layer-cum-step-cum-staircase-cum-spiral-cum-whatever-cum-heights-of-fashion-fail hairstyles, right from 'bedazzled' uniform skirts to exotic variants of 'French braids' – this 'kewl group' is precisely where everything unimaginably stupid began. The girls in the group had guys drooling over them for no

fathomably sane reason apart from their grossly abusive lingo (Yeah, back in those days, that was considered classy and the people who said these on a regular basis were considered divine). The guys in the group had girls killing for them (Perhaps due to serious mental illnesses). And there I was – a mute spectator to all the amazing horizons of human foolishness as the middle-school hormones soared high.

Anyway, moving on with my story, one afternoon, near the canteen, I thought I heard someone whisper my name. Okay, so I wasn't one of the 'kewl group' and didn't endeavour to be, either. Like, ever! And obviously, in the school premises, no one could ever talk of anything other than 'kewlness', so it kind of shocked me a little when I heard my name out in the open. It must be something really huge they were talking about because things like these didn't happen to me every day.

I turned to look in the direction of the whisper. Two of my juniors were pointing at me and saying something of huge interest. Baffled, I just decided to smile at them. But lo and behold! As soon as they saw me looking, they immediately took to their heels and fled down the corridor as if they'd spotted a T Rex in the hall.

I shrugged and walked up to the counter, "One pack of Cheetos please – the orange one,"

The kid at the canteen looked up at me, seemed startled for a while, regained composure, went to the fridge and got me a bottle of Coke instead.

"Er... Sammy, I asked for a pack of Cheetos, not Coke!" Samuel looked up at me sheepishly, grabbed the Coke back and returned with what I had ordered for. I was about to pay up when Samuel said, "No money required, ma'am!"

I stood confounded for a while. What?! No money required? And more disturbingly," Ma'am"? Sammy had always called me "Eve", not even "di"! What the heck was going on here? I swore I would find that out somehow and stormed off (Obviously, without paying! I'm surprised you were even wondering!)

I knew I had had enough. I knew I had to do this. I knew it would take guts. But, it must be done. And I'm not a coward. I had to brace myself enough to enter the dreadful hub of all gossips, the throne of the Gossip Queen: the Girls' washroom!

"What's going on?" I banged in. Everyone inside stood shell-shocked for a while.

"You're dating him?" a curious girl with triple nose rings, double earrings and a lip piercing asked me, tearfully. (Okay, no offence, but how many holes in your body are 'kewl' at one time?)

"Am I?" I was absolutely clueless (and not to mention: aghast)
"You've met his parents!"
"Wow! Really?" (I had no idea what Ms. Holes was talking about)
"You're moving to LA with him?"

"That's fantastic, isn't it?"

"Oh my God! You're engaged then?"

That did it, "Of course I am, Ms. Holes! He gave me a 100 pound diamond ring which just broke my ring finger into a million pieces!" I shouted, pointing towards the small paper cut on that finger.

Deep silence

"By the way, who the hell are you talking about?" I was beginning to get a little uncomfortable.

*   *   *   *

A minute later, as I emerged out of the washroom, I had to try extremely hard not to choke myself with laughter. Turns out Ms. Holes' 'boyfriend' had walked out on her and one of her friends had seen a look-alike of mine (By 'look-alike', I mean: bland black hair, 5"4', simple jeans) 'hanging out' with him. This 'boyfriend' had been the product of the Head of the HR Department of a multi-million dollar enterprise founded in LA and he was shifting back to Los Angeles in a week or two. Hence, all the drama

Not that I minded. The guy was cute and rich, but you know where the problems lay?

1. I didn't know his last name.

2. I had never met him anywhere off the school premises.

3. He couldn't spell 'pneumonia' without at least ten failed attempts.

4. He couldn't add two and two without a calculator.

Thinking long term, these might turn out to be problems when we're educating our kids in LA, right? So I told Ms. Holes not to worry. I would dump him soon enough.

But I admit, I went through hell (in the most literal sense of the phrase) those two weeks before he transferred – with absolutely no fault of mine! Just because I didn't bother to clear up the hot gossips about me that were doing rounds on the premises! Well, that was a fun school gossip I had to handle. But as you grow, the gossips tend to take a turn for the bigger and the worse. Make sure you steer clear because in every place and every phase you're sure to meet some ridiculous people with ridiculous gossips!

*   *   *   *

'The form in which friendships are broken.'
"What is the worst form of gossip you've ever encountered?" I ask Prajit. He seems disturbed by the question.
"You touched a nerve there," I scoff at Anamika.
"Can't you just sit silently for a while?" Anamika screams back at me.
"The form in which friendships are broken," Prajit replied. For a moment, I thought I saw a very distant unrecognizable look in his eyes.
"You can tell me,"

"There was this girl Tanya – an amazing friend and a great person. She was the one who even suggested us to make this club an official one. She had a fabulous drive and motivation, always propelling us to see the brighter side of things, always propelling us to keep moving…" his voice trails off.
"What happened?" I prod.

"Oh, the usual. We used to spend a good amount of time together, thanks to the paperwork for the club. People got talking. That's precisely what people do, isn't it? They talk. We never cleared things out between us. I never lent those gossips a rat's rear. But I guess, she did. Things began to get awkward between us. I never understood why,"

I could relate so well to a certain episode in my life too. It hurt badly. It stung! But that day, I realized something: People have a right to play with words, not with emotions, not with things as important as friendships. So many times you end up giving yourself away to the wrong people just because of something 'people say'! Then, you trip, fall and get bruised.

"How did you know things were wrong?"

"She slowly drew back from me…"

"Drew back as in?" Anamika continued.

Anamika asks that question and immediately bites her tongue.

"Shameless freak, aren't you?" I direct the question at her, "You can see very well that he isn't very comfortable talking about it… Drew back, as in!"

She apologizes, but by then it's too late.

"She drew back from the club in general. She stopped investing her time and her efforts. She stopped investing her energy. She grew wary and cold. She wouldn't be as supportive as she used to; she wouldn't be as candid as she used to; she just became somebody I used to know," he sighed.

The last phrase struck a chord and I recoiled. I didn't want to know more. I understood. And I empathized too well: 'Somebody I used to know'.

*   *   *   *

Blown out of proportion
"Are you on Facebook, Sir?" I ask on our way out, hoping to stay in touch at least over the social networking site, if not through anything else.
"Of course, that's the pulse of the virtual world, isn't it?"
"These days, yes,"
"I've had some crazy experiences over Facebook though," Shan Sir sighs.
"How crazy?"
"Oh, very. Like, one fine day I wake up to find myself trending high. You know the thing that people do with hash-tags these days? I'll show you what a few people had written on my wall," he takes a piece of paper and begins to write:
#soproud of #you
#Youdidit
#Cnt #beleev #u #made #suchhhhhha #breakthru #proud #happy4u

"Oh. My. God!" (I said it better than Janice this time) it burns me up from within to see the plight of the English language. People are tormenting it right in the ICU! It isn't even being euthanized! Such pain.

Dear English,
I promise to attend your funeral whenever you give me the opportunity to.

Regards

"Yeah! That was just... tragic,"
"Why was that tragic? They were just complimenting you on your wall," (regardless of the fact that it would take brutal strength to handle the degree to which the language had been traumatized and disfigured and regardless of the fact that they could have called and not face-walled.)

"Because they had blown something out of proportion. A few days ago, I had marketed a product design, which, even though it was feasible, hadn't really been executed so far. These people (I've no idea where from) were complimenting me on 'project formulation' which was very different from 'project ideation'! Consequently, I began to get 110 calls from a 110 customers asking me to deliver the product to them. Hell! How was I supposed to deliver what hadn't yet happened? I had a great time that day handling a gazillion phone calls, explaining to them that there had been a misunderstanding and telling them I'd inform as soon as the product was ready to be launched. By the time I reached home, I was fuming and tired. Oh! The rumours a few mis-informed people can spread!"

[8]
"HIERARCHY" SHALT BRING THY DOWNFALL

Everyone was against everyone.

Let's be honest, how many of you started at least one club in the attic of your house? Okay, stop smiling! SERIOUSLY! Stop smiling. And now, stop pretending to be embarrassed. Stop blushing. Look into my eyes (*_* - let's pretend these are my eyes) and tell me!

Well, I did.
"Which part of your grossly ambitious and misled brain thinks we are grown-up enough to start a community library?" seven-year-old Aishwarya asked seven-year-old Anamika with her patented 'you've-got-to-be-kidding-me' smirk right under her 'you've-got-to-be-kidding-me' nose.

I fired up. This was a direct insult to me. That's the thing with Aishwarya. She never bothers to disguise the fact that she thinks I'm worthless, never even bothers to mask it! "Look, it wouldn't be that tough, okay?"

"Yeah, we'd just need tons of new books and tons of new equipment, not to mention the tons of permissions sanctioned by our parents and the tons of letters attested by the colony authorities – just that!"

"Hey! We already have the books! We just need to start lending them!"
Aishwarya sighed, "You know you have a hopeless friend to deal with when she thinks she can start a community library with the two hundred books stowed away in some cold, uncanny, dark corner of her cold, uncanny, dark closet,"
Anamika stuck out her chin, "Two hundred is enough!"

Back in those times, I had an un-'messable' will power. I meant what I said.
"Okay, but there are the grown-ups who think we children are never up to any good!"

"Great! Then it's their loss! At least we can start a Book Club for our friends – the people who don't categorize others as 'children' and 'grown-ups' but as 'willing to read' and 'dunderheads'." I meant every word of what I said.

Aishwarya pondered over this for a while. Then, she granted me my wish. Together we cleaned the attic, dragged up the books, arranged them (as) neatly (as we could) and learnt MS Excel.

Two weeks into the plan, we had a set of 'librarians' and this Book Club of ours was a huge success. We'd hold meetings in my bedroom every Saturday to check the progress of the club and everything was perfect... until Anamika decided to be the 'President'. Obviously, everyone supported her at first. It had been her 'brainchild' after all. But that was only 'at first'.

I've seen heaven turn to hell, brain pal! And I mean it when I say that too! Within 2 months, the entire 'Book Club' was a mess, thanks to the President, Vice President, Secretaries and whatevers. Everyone was against everyone. Everyone wanted to be ahead of everyone. No logic worked. No ceasefire appealed.

You know those childish fights we've had over such little Book Clubs are actually just the mini-versions of worse and more corrupted fights we have in the 'real world out there'. It never really ends at childhood. The saga continues. Yes, people get extremely power-drunk and extremely dirty out here. Those snaps and gossips in childhood were so much better because they were so much more honest.

*   *   *   *

I'd survived this when I was a seven-year-old kid.

"We've never let the evil branches of hierarchy take root in Spartans," Prajit tells me, with pride.

"Oh come on! We have a President now!" I suggest,

cheekily.

"Yeah, but that's 'now'. We're long established. We even have the status of a non-profit organization now! Obviously, we'll need a 'President' on paper!"
"On paper?"
"Yeah, solely for official purposes,"
I burst out laughing. The current president would not be very glad to hear this.
"Why do you think that's a great thing to do? I used to think hierarchy distributes workload,"

Prajit looks at me as if I've just morphed from a human being to a gorilla right in front of his eyes, "Hierarchy never, mark my words, NEVER distributes workload. Brains do. Capacity does. Nor does it boost performance. All it does is creates a rift between members of a group. We have never had even the slightest bit of hierarchy creep into the club before we were ready to go 'live' in the most official sense of the phrase."

As it seems, another chapter from VIT tried to approach Spartans to merge with them.

"If there had been hierarchy," Prajit analyses, "No one would have stayed grounded. They would have jumped ships just to make sure they get the most coveted 'positions' in either of the clubs. All people care about today is position, Anamika. This is what our world has come to. If, by any chance, even by a stroke of luck, Spartans had a 'President' back then, that would have been the cause of our downfall,"

I nodded vigorously. I knew exactly what he meant. I'd survived this when I was a seven-year old kid.

*   *   *   *

'It's supposed to mean that I'm a Nixer!'

"Chief Nixer" I read out the title from the business card Shan Sir has just handed me, surprised, "What is that supposed to mean?"

"It's supposed to mean that I'm a Nixer!"
"And what is that supposed to mean?"
"I work at FixNix. That's it!"
"But come on! Aren't you the CEO of FixNix? Why just 'Chief Nixer'? Shouldn't you call yourself the 'CEO, FixNix, Inc.' or something?"
Shan Sir smiled, "Hierarchy ruins even the greatest of enterprises!"
I look at him for a while, amazed, "But how can a company work without hierarchy?"

"It is! FixNix doesn't have a President, Vice President, Security Official, etc. It just has Nixers! But obviously that doesn't mean all of the employees do the same work. It's just that there's no fight over a damned title!"
"How would that help?"

Shan Sir smiled, "VIT has a so-called 'student council', doesn't it?"
I nodded, wondering where this was heading.

"Do you have any idea how much of a political power-play goes into getting into the council?"

"Not too much," I admitted.
"Then you're just a kid, Anamika. Wait and watch... Just wait and watch,"

I scampered away from the topic. It sounded downright spooky to me! But then, it was true. The council members I knew had been great diplomats. It's unfortunate; but we've got to survive in the real world, haven't we?

[9]
INNOVATE

Necessity Accident is the mother of innovation

You know the worst part about VIT?

It is the kingdom of the crows.

VIT Crows are the most important and most unashamed things that ever happened to the university. They rule the place and dear non-VITians, no, I'm not joking. If you ever have a chance to step on our campus, just make way to this amazing place called the Food Court, buy a puff and eat it OUTSIDE the food court. Then, kindly write me a letter to clearly illustrate what happened (and go to the Church or the temple or the mosque or wherever you go for worship, if you are well and alive or meet me at CMC).
What happened to Anamika one morning must have happened to at least 75% of the campus at some point of

their miserable lives.

This girl was just running across the campus to SMV (Chill, it's just the name of a building) for a tragic 8 am class, unaware of what was in store for her that day. She had a puff in hand and while I'd warned her over and over again that it was a huge risk to take, she went against me and later, regretted it bad. Just as she was about to cross the food court, a crow appeared out of nowhere, pecked the puff off her hand, and tied to fly away. Unfortunately for the poor bird, the puff had turned out to be heavier than it had imagined and it tumbled down along with the puff. Aghast and pecked and bleeding, I had no clue as to what had just happened. I tried to escape the scene as fast as possible, tripped right in front of the food court and in front of at least a few dozen people, fell head-first and hit her arm on the bag. As if the day couldn't get any better, it turned out that the bag had remained unzipped all along and all the contents came shooting out like a rocket. Wow! It was turning out to be a fabulous start to a fabulous day!

Goodness knows how, but there had been a CD stuck in the bag since a decade or so probably. The CD too shot out and landed right in front of the bird. The best part was that the bird took one look at the CD, turned and took off to oblivion. I was confused, but the reflex was to get the hell out of that insecure place. After gathering along all that I could, I sheepishly continued on my way, avoiding eye-contact with every passer-by. Later, I tried to make sense of what I'd done. It seems that these birds have an extreme phobia of anything bright, and Mr. Rude Crow couldn't stand the light suddenly reflected off the

CD. I had unwittingly witnessed something that could bring about a revolution in VIT: Something to actually scare the crows away!

Yeah, since then, I always roam with at least one CD in my bag wherever I go (just as a safety measure, you know). While my friends in DU say they roam around with pepper-sprays, I roam around with CDs. Rapists and crows – similar beings, different tactics to handle them.

*   *   *   *

The trigger

As I get more and more engrossed in Prajit's story, questions keep popping out of the blue. Halfway through it, I casually ask, "What was the trigger?"
Prajit is perplexed, "I've been talking to you about hierarchy a few seconds ago and you come up with a totally unrelated query like 'What was the trigger?' Am I supposed to understand that you weren't listening at all or that you were listening with your mind grazing in greener meadows?"

I turn red, "No! It's not what you think! No, all that is fine, hierarchy and the boring stuff..."

"Boring stuff?" Prajit fumes. Uh-oh! Time to address the 'fight-or-flight' situation. It would have done me good to have fled, but tragically enough, I chose to take the brunt anyway.

"NO! I mean..." I begin to explain again.

Instead of turning into a sizzler as I'd expected, Prajit is amused, "Yeah, go on. I'd like to know what you mean."

Ouch! That was icy cold, "Umm... I mean it's not everyone around who even thinks of starting a club one fine dewy morning. What put the idea inside your head? In more genuine terms, WHAT THE HELL WERE YOU THINKING when you cooked up this idea?"

Prajit warms up a little and smiles a nostalgic smile, "I wanted to know how it was like to be a part of a club."

I sit numb for a moment or two, "So do I. I want to know how it feels like to be a part of a club too. But that hardly implies that I'd START one today evening, you see." I try to sound logical.

Prajit laughs, "You could stop with the sarcasm already, Anamika! Well, I used to be extremely interested in autonomous robotics and stuff when I first stepped into VIT. So, like any guy in his so-called 'right mind' would do, I approached the RoboVITics club here. I was a really dedicated learner, you know - never missed a single workshop, never forgot to attend a single event. I almost considered myself a part of that club - until they told me I wasn't. They apparently, did not have 'more space on board'. That phrase killed me a little that day - and on top of that, it made me a little mad. All of a sudden, from this dedicated follower, I turned into a ruthless brat... Rejection does this to the best of us. I knew I could dream crazy, go crazy - after all, I had nothing to lose. In my mind, I'd already lost something I never actually owned in the first place. So I don't really know for sure but I think that one rejection gave me a hell lot of courage. In a minute I was like, 'F*** the world. If they won't take me in, I'll show them what they've lost!' And that, Anamika, was the trigger,"

*   *   *   *

'Find what you want and get that!'

"Sir, you've told me enough about FixNix now. I'm bored," I murmured.
Shan sir laughed, "So what else do you want to talk about then?"
"Tell me about YOU!" I stated, with emphasis.
"What about me?"
"Well, you know, we've been talking about innovation for quite a while now. Tell me some incident during your childhood which made you 'innovate',"

I saw him smile distantly. Something must have struck him. I waited.
"I liked to travel since childhood, you know. But then again, I was an anonymous little kid in an anonymous little village. I couldn't exactly ask Mom and Dad to fund me for a trip to Las Vegas, right?"
"Oh, that's terribly sad," I empathised.

"Yeah, but our anonymous village had this wonderful cricket team. So these cricketers used to roam around the entire state for matches and stuff. But here's another tragedy: I neither liked cricket, nor was I good at it."
"That's brutal!" I agreed.

"So, I decided to go with them on every match they went!"

Wait, what had just happened? Did I miss something? "Umm... Wow, sir, that's fabulous! But WHAT? How could you accompany them on the matches if you neither liked, nor played cricket?"

"I thought about it, that's all. I knew what I wanted. I wanted to travel. I knew what I had. I had a cricket team and a physical existence. Do the math. I decided to be the ball-boy. Simple as that! And boy, I had a great time traveling!"

Talk about making the best of your resources. The next time I want something I can't have, I'm just going to call this person up and ask him to innovate for me!

[10]
JOIN HANDS WITH GRACE

Be polite because they can't deny!

For instance, let me take you to Kolkata.

Once during the Puja season, when I was back there, my brother did something horrible (not like he's usually up to any good, but yet...) My grandparents, cousins, uncles and aunts live extremely close to one another. It's at most a two-minute walk from one house to the next. So, technically, you could even call it a joint family. So just before the Puja, when arrangements for halls, idols, flowers, fruits, paintings, *alpana* and the royal 'Bangali Bhog' need to be made, everyone comes together to create the perfect blend of *moja* (fun), *adda* (gossip) and *chhoto-khato kaaj* (a little bit of work). We Bongs tend to stick to our standards. 'A little bit of work' most obviously implies 'only a little bit of work and no more'. We procrastinate really well, too. So, while to outsiders it may seem that our Puja preparations begin months in advance, insiders know that the real preparations begin only a day or two or at most a week before (Bongs who have any qualms with this sentence are kindly requested to report to me immediately. I'd love to visit your family next Puja!)

Another huge fear that needs to be taken into consideration is our love of food (I'll explain why it's a fear soon). For the Bhog, there are some delectable dishes which any sane human wouldn't dare to refuse. And the problem is: We Bongs are too sane for our own good. Refusing the food isn't even an option to us. Ours is a race against time to save the food till Bhog! A typical *ginni* (Bong homemaker) would have to 'taste' the preparation at least 10-12 times before it's actually ready to be served on a platter and if 10-12 *ginnis* together end up in the kitchen, then you can imagine how much of the dish would be left to be served at the end of the 'tasting sessions'.

So, to make the food last was an evident challenge. On top of that, there happened to be some thoughtless Bong-blooded kids in the house.
The night before Ashtami, the refrigerators were (over)loaded with Mom's highly coveted Chennar Payesh, Chhoto Pishi's mouth-watering Chum-chum, Dida's amazing Mishti Doi and Pantuva, and the omnipresent Roshogolla. I admit it was an inexplicable struggle to stock them in the fridges and not straight in

our stomachs. That night, as my cousins and I cried tears of separation from our beloveds, we went to bed with Hugo's quote in mind: 'Even the darkest of nights have an end'. We waited for our morning to come. If love would make us wait, so be it. We could wait.

Guess what? Love broke us.

The next morning we woke up to an enormous hullabaloo in the kitchen. Someone had stolen the Mishti Doi! I was devastated.

After a hullabaloo which lasted for over 2 hours, it was decided that the store-room upstairs should be checked before someone headed out to buy new tubs. I and El made way upstairs with fingers crossed, our hearts drowning in relentless prayers. What we saw next took away all our faith in humanity and children. The store-room door was locked... From inside! Baffled, we began to knock frantically.

Immediately, Rehan's voice answered from within, "I didn't eat the yoghurt!"

I'd be damned if I said anything less than the fact that at that instant of my life, all of me hated all of him. El began to shed crystal tears of hurt and I just increased the status of 'knocking' to 'banging like a crazed jackass'.

Finally, he emerged with curd stuck all onto his devil-like, ugly, stupid, jerk-face. I felt vendetta sear my veins. For a moment, I thought I even sent those puffs of smoke out of Anamika's ears. And apparently, I must have, because Rehan was backing off like a sheep stuck on an empty farmhouse with a fox. Dragging him downstairs, I informed about the rest of the world about his crime and waited intently for the zombie Apocalypse to befall him. But then, Rehan began his oratory again, which figuratively sounded as lame as this: "Friends, Relatives, Fellow men, lend me your ears for I come here to beg thy forgiveness. I plead guilty of the accusations that have been hurled upon me and I regret my impulse and lack of self-control. But as you can see, I'm just a kid in pain. I hereby promise that I wouldn't do any such thing henceforth. As for this time, obviously, the decision rests in your hands. Punish me if you wish, hit me if you wish, for you're all honourable men..."

What a double-faced hypocrite! He could lure people into letting him go unscathed! He could make people laugh at his antics in the most strenuous of times! Oh, how I loathed him then.

A few days later, on our way to the tennis court, when I'd calmed down a little, I asked him curiously, "Man! How did you manage to get out of that sticky situation I'd so strategically gotten you into?"

He gave me his unnerving shrewd smile, "It's easy... Just remember that when you plead, or advertise, join your hands with grace!"

"Bloody moron!" I chased him with my racquet all around the court.

$$* \qquad * \qquad * \qquad *$$

Helping hands

"I can't even begin to tell you how important a role my

friends and teachers played into shaping us up,"

"Obviously,"
"You understand, right?"
"Yeah, I completely understand: You have communication issues," I smiled, understandingly.
"Can you be serious for once and give me the respect I deserve?"
I try had to conceal a grin which ultimately breaks through, "No,"
"I should have known better. My bad, sorry,"
"It's okay. Mistakes happen,"
"Now before you force me to pick drive a stake through your heart, can we get back to the topic at hand?"

"Yeah, friends – I understand, but teachers? Don't they exist solely to complicate life?"

"No, not all of them, Aniruddh Sir is one person I'll always remember... Always. He was the first person who taught me what it means to be 'caught up in a political web'. He confided in me, taught me to think on the right lines and did everything he could for Spartans. He gave us a forum for publication and production. Our media house would have meant nothing without his constant back-up. Spartans will always be indebted to him..."
"Was he into the media and stuff?"
"No, he sketches, though,"
"Then, why just him?"
"Because some people have the capacity to pull you up from the depths of life with their helping hands,"

* * * *

Making the best of your hands: Partnering with placement centres

"It's all about making the best of your hands," Shan Sir says.

"Like?"

"Like partnering firmly with new fresh talent,"

"New fresh talent doesn't grow on trees, does it? How do you make sure you get the new fresh talent?"

"Well, when it comes to the business world, you'll see that we're always seeking fresh new talent. At every start-up talk I've been invited to, I've never failed to mention the importance of attracting the newbies. That is the reason your university has a PAT centre in the first place! To create the bridge between students and the corporate world. What is essential is to maintain a constant and well-established rapport with the placement centres so that you get a fresh influx of talent every year. I personally also advocate taking in interns. Prajit here worked as an intern with me this summer – and I must say, he was a nice guy to work with,"

I look over at Prajit who seems to be blushing for the first time ever in his life, "Relax, he doesn't really mean it. He's just saying that out of courtesy," I quip, trying to make him a little more comfortable.

"Yeah, I am," Shan Sir joined in. That's all we were going to do this evening. Pull each other's legs. Prajit gave me a killer look which very clearly translated to, "Mind your own business, moron!"

I turned away, satisfied with the reaction.

"Yes Sir, go on," I grin.

"Yeah, so, well, that's about it. Since FixNix was founded in Vellore, VIT has obviously been an integral part since its very conception. I've visited the place plenty of times and had hands-on interactive sessions with the students. You must have heard of the Technology Business Incubator in TT, right?"

For once, I get the opportunity to flaunt my affirmative nodding skills.
"The TBI has helped me a lot with everything. Also, there's a student-run club called the Blueprints' Club if you know. I've been a guest speaker quite a few times there – wonderful kids, I must say,"
'Kids' – The way he calls us kids reminds me of Mom.

"So ultimately, what I'm trying to hint at is that colleges and universities are store-houses of a lot of talent. We entrepreneurs are out here to grab the ones we find best. Partnering with VIT has been one of the best decisions of this journey so far!"

I'm suddenly all proud to be a VITian – forget crow issues, forget FFCS, it was nice to know somebody actually thought we were talented (Our teachers would never admit anyway!)

[11]
DON'T BE ASHAMED TO BE A KID

A section dedicated to Rehan

Disclaimer: Before you read through this, I want you to UN-know these facts:
1. That I turned legit just a few months ago
2. That I still adore Johnson's Baby products
3. That given the opportunity, I'd choose Disney's animated series over Sex and the City any day
4. That I'm the last person on the planet you can accept advice from when it comes to "growing up".

There,

You're now ready to join me on "a brief rendition of the

challenges life throws in your way and how to overcome them with grace". (Phew! Really?)
Or
How to make it Through to Adulthood Alive & without Blowing up the World

So yesterday, I was hanging out with Rehan (over video-calls of course) when I mentioned something about "when I was 10" to which he responded "Wow! Sometimes I forget that you were once a kid... Just like me!" Now, dissecting human psychology and throwing all sorts of maturity into a 5000 metres deep trash can, I found this remark not just disconcerting but downright insulting because it implied to me a couple of things:

- That I was no longer a kid
- That I was so far removed from kid-dom that it was reasonably inconceivable that I was ever once a kid

BASICALLY, that I was an "adult".

Story of my life: Till 11.59 pm (IST) March 25, 2014, I believed that as soon as midnight struck,

- All the barriers that planet Earth had ever put up between me and freedom would come crashing down
- I'll understand everything that I didn't a while ago
- There won't be mysteries anymore
- I'll metamorphose from a larva to a butterfly

But at 12.01 am (IST) March 26, 2014, I realized that none of it could be farther from the truth... So, I stood there, without any crashing of barriers, without any sudden revelations, without any metamorphosis... So great was my trauma that I saw no joy in adulthood anymore. But time is an evil thing. It wouldn't allow me back to kid-dom. Stranded and cold, I waited on the dreamless island of grown-upism.

So when my brother reminded me, I cried out in reply: I DON'T want to be a grown-up!

"But being a grown up is awesome! You get to stay up as late as you want!"
^^ That got me thinking - while staying up late is VASTLY overrated, my life does look a lot different than it did even a year ago. I'm certainly an adult by legal standards. And life is, by no means, WORSE! :D It's just... Different! So bro, since you seem so interested in being an adult, here are 6 things you need to know before 18:

1. Being "adult" has very little to do with your actual age

It's NOT like you hit a certain age and you make it to the destination of adulthood and maturity. Adults are goobers, Rehan! Yes, many of them are wise and awesome - but some of them older than Mom, Dad, Grandpa and Grandma are still silly and act pretty juvenile. They are more ridiculous than the kids in your school who suck the buttons on their jackets. Your age is NOT a free pass (or a hindrance) to Maturity City. I met some adults, some really smart ones! - who seem to perpetually inhabit a realm of teenage drama (including the bits where they lock horns with each other and try their best to bring each other down in public! I could do nothing but laugh at these sweet little grown-up kids). So don't be in too much of a hurry to grow up. Judging by your insight, you're already there (Just drop the pencil chewing)!

2.   The coolest adults are also the most humble and the most thankful - I've learned the most from them.
Unfortunately, there's no correlation between age and the number of mistakes you make. You also never seem to stop growing as a person, regardless of the number of life experiences you acquire. So, while I'm talking to you Rehan, like I'm some seasoned veteran of life, I'll probably read this tomorrow in self-loathing of my pretension. I'm already 18, which effectively makes me a dinosaur in your eyes, but in reality, it hardly qualifies me to speak on adulthood with any degree of authority. But you'll run into people who are curing cancer, have fought in wars, changing the world, and being great fathers, mothers, grandparents and teachers. THOSE are the folks you should be listening to!
2.5   Something that hasn't changed: You should continue to say 'please' and 'thank you'.

3.   You become more aware of how differently people view the world. But no matter how strange a person's beliefs are, they deserve a basic level of respect.
^SO much easier said than done, buddy. But don't forget - in someone else's eyes, YOU're the crazy person.

4.   Adventures start to look a little different.
I have friends who seem to be in a different country each week. And then there's me: Presenting to you the girl who's lived in 2 places her whole life time. People's idea of adventure seem to have evolved (No, do not ask

Darwin to kill me)! I couldn't wait to leave home when I was 17, but now I can see how exciting and crazy and adventure-filled life is, regardless of where you are!

5.   Circumstances often love to meddle with your head.
Whether it comes to your physical, psychological, social or emotional well-being, circumstances just HAVE to be taken into consideration while making decisions. Not "giving a shit about the society and time" is okay to a certain extent. But this is an adolescent-ish strategy. The "Don't think" attitude doesn't work every time. The thing is: I feel as helpless as you do when you know the ball is not in your court anymore. You can't help but laugh things off in your head knowing that letting go is the best you can do. Maybe sometime else (Yes, Expectation and Hope are just kids no matter how grown up you yourself are. Sometime, somewhere, somehow, they still believe in the existence of a rosy world.)

6.   Nobody really knows what they're doing! It's terrifying and simultaneously consoling. It's hilarious!
I used to work at the VIT Community Radio for a while. I kind of discovered then that even the most brilliant professors don't always know how to control the kids! The weirdest thing about growing up is realising that Mom and Dad weren't always right. Grown-ups are still learning, life is funny like that! But Rehan, for our purposes, Mom and Dad are effectively always right. Life is easier if you just listen to them!

Oh! And by the way, just stay calm and let time take its course! Never fall out of love with yourself because however much you grow, you'll still be you!

*   *   *   *

'Follow kids? I AM one!'

"Do you follow kids too?" I ask Shan Sir as I see him toy with the tray just as Rehan does back at home. He reminds me of my brother!

"Follow kids?" he seems to be hurt by the expression as I wonder what I said wrong, "I AM one!"

I heave a sigh of relief. Oh yeah! Now how many people do you find who admit that? And yet, somewhere deep within us, there will always be a child banging to be let out.

"So tell me if you've ever been a kid during your stint as an entrepreneur,"
Shan Sir hesitates for the first time, "I don't know if you're particularly interested in knowing that,"

"I am!" his hesitance makes me all the more curious.
"Well, I've behaved like a kid once and I'm not sure it was the right thing to do,"

"Did you achieve the desired 'end'?"
"Yeah, that I did," he beams.
"Alright then, the ends justify the means. Go on!"
"You are cheeky, aren't you?"
I ponder for a while and then reply, sarcasm oozing out of every word, "I guess not,"
Shan Sir laughs, "Do you know about the NASSCOM?"
"Sir, if only you'd stop asking me to make sense of those words which mean nothing to me, it'd be sort of helpful!"

He smiles, "Aye aye captain, ready to help!"
I stoop to pick the pen that has very conveniently, landed exactly under the centre of the coffee table.

"So NASSCOM happens to be this generous government certified body which helps start-ups to... well, start up. But like everything in India, the application procedure is extremely daunting. The day you finish applying for recognition by NASSCOM, you should treat yourself to a vacation in Hawaii. I, on the other hand, finished applying and actually waited for a reply! Again, like everything in India, the authorities didn't reply. After a few months of futile waiting, I decided to screw them headlong,"
The situation was getting interesting, "What did you do? Call them, perhaps? And give them a good hearing?"
"Call? Oh! That's what adults would do!"
"What did you do then?"

"I directly stormed into one of their conferences, stopped them halfway, and demanded an explanation. I told them I either deserved a straightforward 'yes' or a 'no'. If they were willing to accept the application, they should accept it. And if they weren't, then they could very well reply with a 'no'. But HELL! REPLY! Don't keep me hanging! Now, as you can see, this is precisely how an adult would have reacted to the situation at hand, but the modes of communication would have been different. He'd either have used the e-mail or the phone. Both of these are considered to be the appropriate formal forms of communication. Only a kid would be go off his hinges and climb onto them head-first!"
"How did they react?"

"Well, in front of me, they were all sane and adult-ish and told me they'd 'get back to me'. But I knew I had left an impact on them, thanks to my kid-strategies. They'd remember me. And they better respond as soon as possible. True to my thoughts, respond, they did. I'd barged in on them at 6 pm the previous evening. The following day, at 6 am, I received a mail from them with a confirmation of membership,"

"That was quick!"
"That was quick because I acted like a kid here. Imagine the number of phone calls and e-mails they receive every single day. Had I tried being an adult, I'd still be hanging!"

That was decidedly the best way he could put it!

[12]
LANGUAGES AND LEVELS

Making them 'get you'!
Let me tell you another story:

A random Saturday night:
Sharp 10 pm:
I am at my usual spot (a fortress of pillows) with a cup of freshly brewed coffee, curled up in a warm blanket with my 6-year-old cousin and a big book of fairy tales. I sometimes wonder if I'm a little too old for those bedtime stories now. After all, they do not work in real life anymore, do they? Wouldn't it be better if I just went out for the midnight movie with the rest of my "adventurous" pals?
Somehow, I manage to shovel these thoughts into an insignificant corner of my brain. The optimist in me says, "Find adventure here. She's your sister. You rarely get to

spend time with her. Now that you have it, use it! Don't be a moron!" The pessimist smirks, "What a bore this is! There's nothing you'll get out of it but plain monotony – and perhaps a sleepy sister too. Go for the movie, dunderhead! They've called you up four times over. Just get up and run!"

I steal a glance at my sister hoping she's asleep by now so I can rush out of the temptingly open door. But no, she's (very conveniently) wide awake. She looks at me and giggles like she knows exactly what's going on inside my head. Unfortunately and instantly, I fall prey to her huge, expectant eyes. That is her evil tactic. She knows just how to work my strings by... doing absolutely nothing! "She is mean and innocent and knows how to get things done!" I grumble as I give in to the sweetest smile in the history of mankind. How can any poor sane human refuse a fairy tale to this evil little princess? Trapped and defenceless, I begin to read out from the book,

"Once upon a time..."

An hour later, I finally draw to a close: "And they lived happily ever after..." Phew! That was interesting! Sometimes, it's great to revisit your childhood vicariously! But uh-oh! My sister's still wide awake! In fact, she seems even more fascinated now. I roll my eyes in deep despair and wonder what in the world is wrong with kids these days. They are way too curious for their own good! I pretend I didn't notice her fascination, tuck her in, wish her a good night and quietly tiptoe to the door hoping I can still call up my friends and go for the night out. Just when I am about to step out, she strikes, "Di, what does 'happily ever after' mean?"

Oh God! No! I'm not discussing fairy-tale phrases with my decade-younger sister on a fantastic weekend-night! But I know I have to answer her. I have no choice. I'm destined to doom!

"Don't be silly, El! Don't you know what 'happiness' means?"
She pouts and shakes her head, "I just know the word."
I brace myself for battle, "Okay El! If you must know, happiness is a state of mind characterized by positive emotions ranging from contentment to immense joy. It basically occurs due to an excess of biological fluids which are known as hormones. Once the hormones are released into the bodily system, they excite various parts of the brain which attempt to make it 'feel good'. That's it." I smile.

My sister is now staring at me wide-eyed. She has a "what-the-heck" expression written on her face though she doesn't really know how to express it in words. I smile. That's all I need. I turn back to walk out.
"DI! You understood that I did not understand what you tried to make me understand. You did it on purpose! I'm going to call Aunty now and you'll have to give me a Dairy Milk Silk and explain it to me properly!" she seems to be on the verge of tears. Now it's my turn to shout, "What the heck!" So this girl was serious about the definition of happiness! Now, I feel lost. I have given her the precise definition of the word which she doesn't understand and she is now officially blackmailing me to explain to her something that I have already explained and can't explain any better!

"Umm… El! I'll just go get a glass of water and return in a minute. Then, I'll tell you, okay? Wait a second." I run out of her bedroom and fly into my Mom's, hoping against hope that when I return, my dear little cousin would have fallen into a deep slumber.

"What's it, baby? You look flustered!" Mom exclaims.
"Baby"? I whizz around to check if El had followed me. No. She hadn't.
"MOM! Stop calling me 'baby'! I'm 15! I'm old enough to take care of myself!"

Mom laughs an irritating laugh that reminds me that I'll forever be a 'baby' to her, "What's it, my oh-so-grown-up baby? You look flustered!"
This time, I choose to ignore the adjective, "Mom, how can kids be so stupid? They just don't seem to understand anything at all!"

"If you just tell me what El said, perhaps I could get a hang of it," she smiles.

"She's asking me the meaning of 'happily ever after'! What do I tell her?"
"What DID you tell her, dear?"

I repeat to Mom my vain efforts to explain 'happiness' to my sister. A moment of silence ensues in which I try to make sense of her inscrutable expression (and fail miserably). Then all of a sudden, she bursts out laughing. Okay, so if everyone wants to mystify me today, so be it. I put on an eternal scowl on my face and decide to storm out of the room.

"WHAT exactly were you thinking when you recited the definition of 'happiness' from Wikipedia to a six-year old?"

I stare blankly into oblivion, "What else am I supposed to tell her? That's the only definition of happiness I know!"

Mom pulled me close, "How can YOU be so stupid? Don't you know any other definition of happiness? Get down to her age. Get into her shoes. See the world through her eyes. And then, define it! What do you see?"
I start fiddling with my fingers. I decide to take it cautiously, one word at a time, "Happiness is setting the butterflies free from the net. Happiness is rolling down the green meadows in the evening even though I know Mom will scold me later for the grass on my clothes. Happiness is watching the sun return to where it came from. Happiness is when my Pooh bear hugs me every night. Happiness is a whole new story of magic. Happiness is when Snow White wakes up from her coffin. Happiness is when Mom kisses me 'good night'…"
Mom smiles a knowing smile, "Now you see it!"

I give her a bear-hug and set off to El's room… and emerge victoriously with a smug smile on my face.
"Satisfied, eh?" Mom looks at me quizzically.

"Mom, how did you do it? I didn't know what to tell her and then you came along and made me realize where I was going wrong? How can you be so… epic?"

Mom laughs, "It's not 'epicness' dear. It's just the way

you handle things. Now that you say you're 'growing up', do you know what it ultimately means?"

I think for a while. True, I don't. I mean, I know I'm growing up because people say I am. Ritu Aunty looks at me and tells me I've become taller, prettier and more 'lady-like'. Purvi Aunty tells me I've 'grown up' because I now know how to boil rice without pouring water all over myself and getting burnt. Anushri, my classmate, tells me I've 'grown up' because I finally understand how babies are made. Sukriti Ma'am tells me I've become more responsible and 'mature' in handling my studies because I scored a 100/100 in my biology quiz. But, what does all this really mean? I shake my head. I'm baffled! I don't personally know what 'growing up' means!

Mom makes me sit on her bed, looks straight into my eyes and begins to explain, "It means you can now adapt yourself to people, circumstances and their needs. You can now understand who understands what and what words you have to choose with different people to explain the same thing! If you are a kingfisher and you have a few fish friends who ask you the meaning of 'happiness', you cannot really tell them that 'happiness' is flying off the cliffs, over the world and circling the shores of the Great Lakes during sunrise. To you, yes, that is happiness. But you cannot expect the fish to make sense of that! To them, happiness is swimming in the deepest waters and discovering coves that no other species can ever even dream of finding! Now that you're growing, you need to be a little more considerate to people's needs and desires. You need to be able to put yourself in their place and see things through a thousand different perspectives. Realize that what is real and right to you, may not be real and right for someone else. This is the basis of effective communication, understanding and diplomacy – three of the most essential weapons you'll need to face the 'grown-up' world."

    *   *   *   *

This is an incident that took place a couple of years ago. There is absolutely nothing extraordinary about it. It happened on an ordinary Saturday night under ordinary circumstances in the presence of ordinary people – not a trace of adventure. But for some weird reason, I remember it with extraordinary clarity. For some weird reason, that day flipped me over. For some weird reason, it had a profound impact on my thought-processing network. For some weird reason, it taught me things I can never afford to forget. For some weird reason, it played its little role into shaping me into who I am today.

And guess what? I never regretted not going for the midnight movie…
Because for some weird reason, sometimes, it's just worth missing a night-out!

    *   *   *   *

[13]
LAN MARK YOUR COMPETITORS

'I need orange pens'
"Mom, I need orange sketch-pens," Rehan announced on the breakfast table one fine morning.
"Eat," Mom replied coldly.

She has this tendency to go on conversation-strikes for days together (which Dad loves, but that's supposed to be personal, right Dad?) when she's pissed off with something. A conversation-strike is defined as a spell of incredibly short sentences and ear-splitting silences including 'Yes', 'No', 'Eat', 'Go' and 'Die'. Basically, everything gets answered in monosyllables. And believe me, it's the scariest thing in the history of Mom-kind. It makes me cringe.

But apparently, my brilliant brother's brain is even better. Sometimes he reminds me of the relentless spider in the Robert Bruce story who keeps spinning the web until he actually makes it! Only difference: Mom isn't exactly the benign Bruce. Instead of being a patient onlooker, she may just explode anytime and squat the spider down!

"Mom, I need 2 orange sketch-pens, and one orange glitter pen," Rehan seemed to be enjoying it all. This family is full of tight-rope walkers! Mom glanced at him – the 'you-know-I-can-beat-you-to pulp' glance. Just as Anamika was about to get up and get the camera from the cupboard, Dad waltzed in to save the day! I admit, that was one of the most disappointing points of my life! Just when I thought I had a movie, lo and behold! The knight in shining armour appears out of thin air and clears up all the drama!

"Why Rehan? What for?" it kills me as to HOW Dad can keep his calm in front of such a detestable kid he has accidentally transferred his genes to.

"To write names on the board," is the answer.

"What names?"

"Names of kids like me, you know?"

He was being vague on purpose! My sweet little brother was doing this to annoy the hell out of everyone around him. Let me tell you this, brain pal: If I had been in Dad's place, by now, any of the following things could have happened:

1. His head could have been chopped of and flung into some far off desert where it could dry in bliss

2. All his hair could have been distributed evenly

between his two hands
3. He could have been allowed to bathe in boiling oil for 10 minutes (marinate would be a better word-choice here)
That's all.
But anyway, getting back to what Dad said: "Why do you need orange pens for that? Blue will do just fine!"
I couldn't fathom any logical explanation brilliant Rehan could give to that.
But he began, "No, Dad, you don't understand. Blue is a very cool colour. I want orange to mark the people I should be wary of! It's a combination of red and yellow. Both of these are hot colours. Red stands for enemies and yellow stands for friends. Orange stands for those people who are a combination of enemies and friends!"
"How can enemies ever be friends?" even Dad was flabbergasted.
"Oh! They can! Those enemies are called 'competitors'. Sometimes, you need to partner with them. At other times, you need to be ahead of them!"
I was stunned into silence. When will Rehan ever stop giving me such vivid life advice at every breakfast I have with him? It gives me an extra-ordinary inferiority complex!

*   *   *   *

"They call it co-opetition in the business lingo," Shan Sir says, still fidgeting with the coffee-tray and still managing to amuse me with it.
"That's a nice word," I wonder aloud, carefully studying the forensic etymology of the term, "Do you co-opete often?"

"Of course I have to. It's not like I have a choice here. Partnerships have to be forged with your strongest and most vengeful competitors for better product and service quality. The aim is to form the best possible for the worst possible problem. That is what draws the market,"

"But how do you trust your co-opetitors? They may turn out to be complete..." (I scan my brain for a better word which doesn't have to be censored)
"Jerks?" Shan Sir helps.
"Yeah, that's a better word, I guess,"

"You don't have to be able to trust them with your entire company, do you? You just need to make sure they are as dependent on you as you are on them. If there is even a slight fluctuation in the dependency levels, then it may (and most probably WILL) create tons of problems. It's inevitable!"
I switch over to my 'past-memories-related-to-this' mode.

Last year, at VITMUN '13, I'd represented Kuwait at the General Assembly (DISEC) and although I'd been a passive spectator for most of the part, one of the points of the final resolution had still had a profound impact on me. The agenda was the "Reallocation of funds from the military budget towards alleviation of poverty". I don't remember the exact words but the final proposal said that wars between the nations could be ceased if they were made inter-dependent. For instance, if Saudi Arabia began to exchange oil for coffee from Brazil (let's just say. These two nations aren't fighting currently and have no reason to either. But hypothetically, let's assume that they were. Disclaimer: This, in no way, intends to create war mentalities. I'm not instigating anyone or insinuating anything. Don't even dare to read too deeply into this.), then it would not only improve world trade, it would even enhance international relations and also stop wars (because hell! They need each other!) It is a win-win all the way!

That's precisely what Shan Sir was trying to explain...

[14]
SAY 'NO' WITH GRACE

"But so often, Indian families just refuse to understand!" I exclaim in dismay as I redirect to the clutter I'd strategically positioned myself into when I'd told my parents that I wanted to try at shot at Cornell University, USA after XII. Mom, who was usually rational about things, burst into a flood of horrifying tears. I was bewildered beyond compare.

"Quick, do a re-run of what you just told her," Anamika commanded me, certain that I must have said something like, 'Mom, I want to work with the Taliban,' instead of 'Mom, I want to attend Cornell,'

I did as I was asked to. I replayed every word (bit by bit, with the pauses included) until she was convinced that I'd said 'Cornell' and not 'Taliban'.

Finally, I summoned enough courage to ask her, "What's wrong Mom?"

She sniffed through her tears, closed her eyes and prayed for me, "Oh Mighty Lord! Forgive her sins, for she doesn't know what she does,"

Okay, so this was how the drama was destined to begin... Game on!

"Er... Mom?"

"Sit down here and wipe your head, my dear. You need to be really calm as we think this through," I wondered if this was addressed to me or to her own self, "Yeah, so look, you want to study in a place as... as nonsensical as the States?"

"Mom, nonsensical? It's an Anamika League university! It's supposed to be way better than any of the colleges India has ever had!"

"But do you have any idea about the culture there? The clothes they wear are one-third of the ones you're wearing right now!" she shouts, pointing at the old pair of jeans I was wearing, "And if that's not bad enough, they tear and scratch and crease those too!" she added, perhaps referring to the trend of ripped jeans.

"They eat boiled potatoes and onions and tomatoes with cheese and bread and call that 'burger'. I don't think they've ever even heard of our coveted 'Navratan Korma' or Butter Paneer Masala. They lie around drugged and sedated in front of... what's that word again... oh yeah, 'pubs' and call that 'night-life' when in reality, they're anything but alive. And worse, they sleep around with a dozen people every week and consider it 'fun'! How are you ever going to adjust to the culture-shock? I don't want you to turn into... Into... (Stifled cries)... Into one of them!" she finishes.

Oh! So that was where the problem lay. She thought I'd 'turn into one of them' and return home with a few dozen bottles of booze and a *(let's not even say the word)* guy?! After a month of rigorous insisting, pestering, cribbing and a marathon crying session, I finally lost my peace. Neither was she willing to listen to my explanations, nor were her explanations making any sense to me! So we dragged Dad into picture.

Remember that clichéd childhood phrase you used to tell Dad when Mom denied you something? I used the same, "Dad, she's not even letting me explain! Please make her understand!"

"Let's see," was Dad's patent reply (since I was 3)
After a bedroom hearing-session which lasted over three hours, it was judgement time. I had my fingers crossed and promised God that my belief in Him would be reinstated hundred-fold if only he let me have my way this one time. "Deliver me!" I cried over and over again.

For a few minutes, everything was quiet and my frustration had come dangerously close to its exploding limit, with 'High voltage, keep away' sign flashing in fluorescent red.

"Sumi, that's an invalid argument," Dad states blankly. I stand mesmerized, hoping fervently that the judgement ended there, "But..." Dad broke my heart with that word,

"The conclusion is correct,"

I felt the ground slip away from beneath Anamika's feet and I also felt myself fall thud on the floor and break her nose (figuratively of course. Physically, no one was injured though. That's the worst part. People see what the body goes through, not the scars I've borne), "What do you mean?"

"I mean, Anamika, let's think logically," I didn't want to! But he went on (who cares about what I want anyway!), "Cornell is doubtlessly a wonderful place for an undergraduate, but have you ever wondered about the finance? It's a private university in Ithaca, USA. Do you really think we can afford to send you there with absolutely zero financial security? How much do you think it costs? The price of a Melody?" (Apparently, this is the new currency in India. The 'Anna' at the store near the Ladies' Hostel deals in 'Melody's; the 'Akka' at the TT photocopy shop deals in 'Melody's; even the auto-rickshaw 'Anna's here in Vellore deal in 'Melody's. Let's just wait a bit. The Indian Government should accept it as a valid form of payment soon enough and then perhaps, we'll have 'Melody's pouring out of ATMs and hear vendors on streets shouting "20 Melody's a piece!", "50 'Melody's a piece!")

Unfortunately though, Dad's argument made sense to me. I understood what he was trying to say (and Anamika officially hated me for it, but oh, well...) I honestly couldn't afford to spend so freaking much on an undergrad degree. I couldn't go there without a scholarship. Well, there goes...

Later, when I reflected on it, I figured out something Dad did, which Mom didn't. He just said 'No' in a way that convinced me that it would really be better off NOT to do what I was thinking. He just reasoned it all out. Mom telling me that I shouldn't go to Cornell because I'd get baked and wasted made little sense to me because I knew I was strong enough to bar myself from such strong unnecessary external influences. But Dad telling me I shouldn't go to Cornell because of it wouldn't be economical made perfect sense to me because I knew this was a factor that wasn't under my control!

*   *   *   *

"You've networked so much! You must have had some people-trouble!"
"Networking has never been the tough part, Anamika. It's never talking and connecting that's tough. It's saying 'no',"

"And why would you have to say 'no'?" I immediately realise what a foolish question that must have been.

During GraVITas '13, the Spartans couldn't conduct any official event because unfortunately, now they knew about the DSW and all the permission issues. But that didn't mean that they'd rest in peace doing nothing at all. Somehow, they conducted two very successful events on September 15th, the second day of GraVITas '13 (which also happened to be Engineers' Day), but they couldn't use the GraVITas logo. So they had to conduct them in association with some other club in VIT. This is when they first realised that they needed to get the paperwork done as soon as possible to avoid further drama. But reluctantly, for that one time they agreed to merge their events with a separate club.

"This turned out to be quite a wrong move," Prajit reflects.

"Why would you say that? At least it allowed you to conduct the events in the first place!"

"Yes, but later, when we were trying to set up VIT Spartans with the office, with stamp-paper, separately, as an autonomous club on campus, there were issues with this other club which had once helped us. They had expectations of merging, apparently,"

"Uh-oh!"
"That was an extremely sensitive time. We couldn't afford to ruin links with them. Nor could we afford to sever all contact. Also, we didn't particularly want to merge with them. Come ON! That had been the point all along – making a completely separate body of enthusiasts. We couldn't just leave them without a reply. That would be ungrateful on our part. By God, we had a tough time deciding what and how to tell them what we wanted,"
"What did you tell them?" I asked, eyes glinting with curiosity.
"Back of, woman! That's not something I can tell you. You're dangerous. You'll put it down for the world to read,"

I grimace, "So?"

"So the point is: Some things are not supposed to be revealed to outsiders," he winks.

"So you think I'm an outsider now!"

"You aren't. But not every one of your readers would be an insider you see?"

I agree half-heartedly (But let me tell you, dear brain pals: whatever Prajit says is secondary. You'll always be special to me!)

"But that experience really taught me some tact," Prajit continued, "It's all about saying 'no' with grace!

[15]
SKIN OPEN SOURCE
(AND DEMOCRATISE TOO)

"We've talked quite a bit about competitors now. How do you actually figure out who your competitors are? They may be camouflaging too, right?"
"Yeah, of course. They could try, but chances are they'd hardly succeed,"
"Why?"

"Because in the virtual world, we have something called open source,"
I'm immediately reminded of poor Dad who had once tried to explain open source to me and had failed miserably. (But yeah, finally, I'd learnt what it was (and absolutely nothing more).)

"You track your competitors on open-source? That's a smart move!"

"Not really. It's an essential move. The open source usually contains all the ideas that have been or are currently being worked upon. So, it serves multiple purposes. Obviously, to survive in the market, you have to stay updated about the latest bits of information and advancement in your specialty. So that's what this open source does. It helps you find solutions to the problems you encounter and also helps you democratise your solutions to the rest of the world. That's another way of networking and that also gives you an edge to what is happening where in the cyber-security world. The 'who' obviously follows," Shan Sir winks.

"But then people say that you should keep your ideas to yourself as long as possible. What would you say to that?"

"I would definitively call that 'rubbish',"
"That's a pretty strong statement,"

"Of course it is! And I've got evidence to prove why I said what I said," he seems to be in a question-word mood today, "If you keep your ideas to yourself, it just implies that you don't let yourself out in the open either! That in turn means your outreach is low, which again means that few people know about you. Now, if fewer people know about you, then tell me how they'll approach you when they encounter an issue which requires your services? They won't! So you lose customers and in fact, end up throwing the chances on

the face of your competitors!"
"So do you advocate selling of ideas?"

"Not vague ideas – not things that could have been tried if certain situations had crept up. But yes, I whole-heartedly advocate selling of concrete ideas. That is how people see you. That is how people recognize you! You can't sit in a hollow all your life and cry that you're unable to experience the sunlight. If you want to experience the sunlight, you have to get out of your cave, shun all fear of people stealing your ideas and revel under the Sun!"

*   *   *   *

[16]
OF PERSEVERANCE AND PERFORMANCE

Authors are self-obsessed jerks

ll the successful people I know have one thing in common: They are pests. And they never get tired of bugging everyone (including their own selves).
Just yesterday I was talking to this author friend of mine, when I naively asked him, "Is it very difficult to get published?"

"Yes, it is, but eventually, everything will be set straight,"
"Did you publish at the first go?"

"ARE YOU KIDDING ME?"

"But you write so well! I thought you, of all people, must have published at the first go!"

"Yeah, I agree I write really well," (He's flipped the word called 'modesty' straight into some faraway trash), "but that doesn't mean I got people to agree with me on that at the first go,"
"So how many times were you rejected?"

"Just 16."
I gasp, "Sixteen?! Isn't that terrible for you?"
"Ha! Terrible for me? Here I am, pitying all the publishers who've rejected me, and you think it's terrible for me? Come on, Anamika! Admit it! It's terrible for all those publishers who had the chance to take me in, but ended up losing me. I gave them a chance. They didn't take it. Now obviously they'd regret it soon enough,"
I cut the call in utter shock and glance over at Diya who's watching the hundredth episode of F. R. I. E. N. D. S on her depressed little laptop, "Authors are self-obsessed jerks,"
She pulls the earphones out, "Ha! I'm so glad you finally admitted it!"
"I thought you weren't listening!" I seethe.
She doesn't comment, just puts the earphones back on.

*   *   *   *

Digging roots
"So why didn't you just give up in the very beginning?" I ask, shamelessly. I knew I might have. So many financial

110

issues, so many societal norms broken – it sure wasn't easy!

"Anamika... Have you heard of this bamboo tree?"

I nod, clueless as to where bamboo trees were used in cyber-security.

"Do you have any idea how they grow?"

I want to nod, but I don't. If he was asking me about it, it must be different from the way other plants grew and I guess I wouldn't know. (How many of you have done this?) So, I presume it's best to keep silent.

"For the first few years, they do not even begin to come out of the soil they've been sown in! The farmer who chooses to sow these seeds has to hear a hundred-and-one taunts from his neighbours who sow crops in quick rotation. But then, when the roots have dug deep and strong enough, they shoot up. They shoot up so high that they cross every other cash crop that's sown around here! When that happens, the neighbours of the farmer keep staring in envy, for there is nothing else they can do but stare,"

I see where this is heading, "You're a bamboo tree!"

"I believed I was!" Shan Sir laughed.

"What happened then?"

"Nothing... Well, I still believe I am. Just that the roots are still digging!"

[17]
THOU SHALT NOT QUARREL OVER PETTY ISSUES

(Thou shalt not cat-fight)

Okay, agreed that it takes quite some effort to maintain composure when you have people like *censored names* in front of you. The sheer effectiveness of their brains makes you take a deep breath, count till 10 and question God about the future of mankind. But remember folks, you NEED a façade to survive in this world. You can't really bare your true thoughts to every second person you meet! Else, you'll end up baring your teeth too often too!

I'm not asking too much of you, you know? You don't have to be Kristen Stewart to stay expressionless (though, if ever you have the opportunity to take a few extra classes from her, don't you DARE miss it!) But I know friends who phase out because one of them 'wasn't important enough' to the other. This is again due to over-thinking (Ultimately, as you might have observed every bad decision on the planet occurs due to over-thinking. We brains are wonderful things!)

Know about those incidents which look hugely disastrous when dissected and sent for post-mortem examinations at the minuscule level, but turn out to be hilarious in the long run? Two years down the lane, you cry tears of stupidity whenever you recall them, but right then, in the heat of the moment, you end up saying or doing something so hurtful that it wrecks your relationship all at once.

I was once stupid enough to lose a friend over a meeting! Here it goes:

Ayush (over phone): I thought you said you'd meet me once when you came to Kolkata.

Anamika (guiltily): Yeah Ayesha, but this time, the schedule was so packed I couldn't do anything I wanted to and couldn't meet anyone I knew. All this running around the city had seriously taken a toll on me. Please understand, will you?

Ayush: Time will never BE, Anamika! You have to MAKE it! I was waiting for you at McDonald's!

Anamika (guiltily again): I know, dear. But I seriously couldn't meet anyone important. First I was cooped up inside the publishing house. And then, it started pouring cats and dogs. I wanted to see you one last time on campus, but I couldn't! I'm sorry!

Ayush: No, you're not.

Anamika: Ayush, come on! Next time, for sure.

Ayush: You shouldn't really make promises to people who you're too busy for... (His voice broke)

Anamika: I'm genuinely sorry! From the core of my existence!

Ayush cut the call and didn't pick up... Ever again.

I tried contacting him thrice after that. But he'd grown cold and distant and then, it just made me sad to talk to him. So I finally had to give up. But sometimes, I still wonder if he ever thinks of me anymore. I wonder if he has ever picked up the phone to call me as many times as I've picked up mine to call him and put it back down. I wonder if he cares anymore. I wonder if he's never thought of accepting my apology. I wonder if he will ever come back to being friends with me.

I don't have answers to any of these questions, but I know for sure that if our friendship had meant anything to him, he wouldn't really have quarrelled this hard! I'm still waiting for his return...

*   *   *   *

Entertaining fights

"You wouldn't believe the kind of fights we've picked up around this place," Prajit tells me, staring at a couple who are currently in the middle of World War III, on the middle of the road.

"I can very well see that," I grin.

"This is nothing," he turns to me, "We've had epic fight sessions which rival the violence in... (he thinks for a while, trying to come up with a good comparison) in the Lok Sabha Assembly!" Oh God! What has Indian politics come to!

"Oh, that would make a great story!"

"That's all you care about, eh?"

"Yeah, kind of,"

"That's true though. It would make a great story! There used to be this guy named Nagesh in our team,"

"Used to be?" I ask, "Where did you bury him?"

"Okay, I'm sorry! IS, fine? Don't be a grammar Nazi,"

Well, I wasn't... Till people began to kill other people around me. I've come to that stage of life wherein I've officially and for all practical purposes, stopped reacting to that comment.

"Go on," I'm bland.

"So Nagesh broke off from our team after the very first event: War of the Rhymes and started a page of his own. And then, a few members of Spartans couldn't digest the fact that he had done 'something like this' and they decided to direct their personal vendetta toward this one poor guy. I must say I pitied him at one point..." Prajit laughs.

"You weren't angry with him?"

"Why should I be? What had he done wrong? If he thought he was better off starting something on his own, who was I to hold him back?"

"That's true," I agreed.

"But the fights that followed were seriously entertaining,"

"That's because you were out of the battle-field!"

"Yeah, that, in fact, made it all the more enjoyable! When you're out of the ring, you can clearly see that the people inside are fighting over a lost cause, or worse, a non-existent cause! I seriously never understood the logic behind picking up such fights which lead to nothing and unnecessarily sour relations!"
Of course, none of us do!

[18]
RISE ABOVE THE PAIN-INFLICTORS

Get real!

"I never realized it would affect you so much, Anamika! It wasn't even a relationship. It was just a year-long crush. How could you pin your hopes on something as minor as a crush?" Naina smiles as she hands Anamika the twenty-seventh tissue.

"I – I never realized it either, until it did! It did affect me this much Naina! When he said he'd make time to see us when he came around, I thought he actually meant it! When he texted that he'd call, I thought he wasn't kidding! I waited! Why do they say things they don't mean? It's just crazy! I always do this to myself! I think too much about somebody who doesn't give a f*** about my existence, I get my hopes all up. And then I expect that I'd mean as much to him as he does to me! Why is it always that I put worthless people at the top of my priority list and neglect the worthwhile ones who deserve to be at the top? Why is it that I always have scrambled priorities? Why is it that I end up hurting the people who care so deeply for me and put all the fake people on a pedestal? And above all, why do we always fall for the wrong people?" I sniff and look sympathetically at the dustbin I've just filled with all that tissue.

I pause, "Oh my goodness!" I recall, "I've even wasted two hours of my life writing an e-mail to him! Even that doesn't seem worth it now! WHAT HAVE I DONE with my life?"

Naina understands, like she always does, "It's because of towering expectations, Anamika. In reality, you'll never 'fall for' anyone if you truly knew them. EVER! Every guy you meet has some flaws you can never even begin to accept! You just fall over and over in love with the image of the Prince Charming you have in your head. So you try to find the people who resemble your Prince Charming to the closest. But get real, kid! I didn't want to be the one to break this to you, but you don't live in a fairy-tale world, dear! It's harsh, but it's true. The point is that when we get attached to someone, we begin to expect the world from him. We expect him to be super-sensitive to our needs and expectations. We expect his life to revolve around us. But baby, it all goes down the gutter! It's all just an illusion. Forever is a lie. Promises aren't meant to be believed in when they include the word 'forever'. Remember the time when you were in

kindergarten and you told your Dad that this was the very LAST candy you were asking to buy in your entire lifetime? Remember the way you thought you actually meant it? Remember the way Dad smiled as he nodded? He KNEW your 'entire lifetime' currently referred to the next five minutes. Yet, he agreed. Imagine what would have happened if he'd actually believed you!"
"He wouldn't have been Dad!" I laugh.

"Exactly, that is the point! Nothing in life is supposed to be taken too seriously. If you do, it will keep breaking you! Live in the present. Know that hopes, expectations and promises of the future as blurred and foggy as a... as a Delhi winter!" she ends on an incoherent note.
"How do I get over this now?" I sulk.

"Just ask yourself if it was even worth wasting so many tissues over someone who clearly puts you below the 20th position in his priority list. Or worse, doesn't even have a priority list! Duh! Buck up girl! You're hurting the tissues!"

I laugh. I knew now that it wouldn't do to be so sensitive on planet Earth. I had to develop thicker skin. And the moment I knew that, the skin started building on its own!

*   *   *   *

Chromosomes, bank balance and debts
"Do you guys break up in the business world?" I wonder aloud, and then immediately regret the question. It's not like I had to get all formal with Shan Sir, but well, you know, image issues... (All of us are so insecure with

'elders'!)

He pretends like that is the most natural and obvious question I could have ever asked and like he'd been expecting it all along, "Yeah, well, every once in a while... when the going gets tough, and we have trust issues,"

One look at him confirms my worst fears: He wasn't joking!

"But I'm sure it's different from the crap we have to deal with,"

"Excuse me, miss! Says who?"

Okay, so here I was, in the middle of nowhere, drinking coffee with an entrepreneur I had just met a few hours ago, and discussing guy-trouble with him. I feel blessed. How much more does my life have in store?

"Says... all of us!" I retort, ruefully representing the case of all the disappointed females of the world, "At least you don't have to deal with defective chromosomes!"

"Defective chromosomes?"

"DUH! The Y chromosome has innate insensitivity defects. Thank your stars that at least you're saved from a genetically troubled species,"

Shan Sir laughs aloud, "Yeah, perhaps. But we do have to deal with defective bank balances and defective debts - that's almost the same. Actually Anamika, we are surrounded by pain-inflictors from all angles. In the business world, they come in the form of 'partners' (that's not a very surprising term, is it?) The moment the needs, demands, income and expectations from one partner begins to exceed or overshadow those of the other, companies have to part ways. So, it's always safer to maintain a distance and concentrate more on strengthening YOUR company first. It may sound selfish, but that's the way it has to be. Partnerships remain healthy only when both parties know where to stop. There exists a line to sharing of information. I know a few start-ups that failed because they became too dependent on some other pre-established institution. It's like they say: Make friends who are compatible with you. A start-up with two founding members simply CANNOT afford a viable business partnership with, say, Microsoft. It's not because Microsoft is not helpful or anything close; it's just because Microsoft can 'gobble' them up!"

"But what do you do post break-up then?"

"You cry for a while, hit hard on the cold floor, wipe your tears, whine about it for a while, realise that technically, you're still alive and you have all your body-parts just as you used to, get back up and laugh it off a few years down the lane!"

"I was talking business here," I offered, generously, assuming he had misinterpreted my question for something more personal.

"I replied business there," he smiles, "It's not as different as you seem to think it is. Whatever happens, you have to keep your cool and keep moving. Oh, and do not forget to make peace with the companies you broke up with. It's not like you have to rebuild the partnerships, but make peace all the same. It will help you maintain your sanity and not go crazy with hopes of vendetta. You have to rise above all that to truly succeed,"

[19]
DON'T BE A SHEEP IN A HERD

(Or if you absolutely LOVE being sheep, at least be a black one in a herd of white!)

Okay, so yesterday, I was randomly chatting up with Naina and we had Youtube open in a tab. Her 3 GB WiFi quota (weird hostel rule #1001) was far from drained and we were hopelessly jobless. So, as any sane college-goer can easily deduce, we ended up wrapped in unwashed bed-sheets with a bucket of popcorns and dimmed room-lights. Wandering aimlessly all over the internet, we came across a channel called IISuperwomanII.

Four hours and 40 videos later, we were still clutching our stomachs and rolling on the floor laughing.

"That was a lot of awesomeness cramped into one channel!" Naina announced.
"Sure was!"

Later that night, I got busy at my gym. This 'IISuperwomanII' girl had some seriously super brains. She had made a hell lot of fame by just cashing in on the powers of the internet! And unlike the usual herd of e-commerce worshippers, she'd created a genre of her own! She wasn't selling any material product through e-commerce; she was selling smiles! She didn't own any one of the million brands up online; she was a brand herself! This is where the difference lay. She could have been a sheep in a herd. Well, she almost was. But at least she was a black sheep in a herd of white! And goodness, that bought her some name.
Oh, PS. If you haven't yet watched any of her videos, go! Go right after you're done with this book. You'll (hopefully) love it! Yeah, yeah, you're welcome!

*   *   *   *

"The problem with this generation of entrepreneurs is that they cannot think beyond e-commerce!" Shan Sir sighs.
"So what's wrong with e-commerce? It's easy, it has a virtual existence, it simplifies things so much! Our current writers on the topic of entrepreneurship worship e-commerce!"
"Everything about e-commerce is just perfect – apart from the fact that we've become limited to it! I'm not saying e-commerce needs to be banned. All I'm telling

you is that we need to dare to think beyond it. It used to be a novel idea before it got all mainstream. Personally, I don't think it sounds appealing anymore. It doesn't hit!"

That's true. Only some do. My respect for IISuperwomanII just increased 10 fold after this conversation.

*   *   *   *

We're decentralised

"Why do you think you got an overwhelming response to your club as soon as it was put down on stamp-paper and sealed?"

I'm currently an editor on the VIT Spartans page and we receive at least 5 new messages asking us the procedure to get into the club every single day! It's humbling to read through the messages.

"I cannot tell you for sure, Anamika, but I think it was because we were different. We stuck out. You see, every other club in VIT is dedicated to one single thing or another. We have the Dance Club for dancers, the Music Club for musicians, the Dramatics club for... well, people like you, the Debate Society for debaters, and while they are all excellent performers, they are dedicated to just one thing. We, on the other hand, do everything! We're decentralized,"

"Do you think that's a very good thing, though?" I sound sceptic to my own self!

"I don't know if that is necessarily a good thing, but yes, it's different! That is what caught attention. We have 5 divisions under Spartans itself and if you ask me, that's a huge step to take,"

[20]
TAKE SOME TIME OFF TO LIVE OFFLINE!

So, what are your plans for the evening?

When was the last time you played football in the rain? When was the last time you went on a road trip? When was the last time you went camping? Have you ever been in a caravan? When was the last time you climbed a hill? When was the last time you swam and splashed around in the sea? When was the last time you rolled on the beach?

When was the last time you put your video game down? When was the last time you unglued yourself from the television? When was the last time you checked your phone? When was the last time you survived without an air-conditioner? What is the "last seen" status of your

WhatsApp account? When was the last time you "logged off" from the virtual world and set foot on the real one?

Yesterday, I asked Rehan (over the phone) what his plans for the day were. Here's the whole conversation succinctly put for you:

I: So, what are your plans for the evening?

My brother: I'm just thinking off playing for a while, that is, until Mom starts giving me sermons on the importance of studies and studious kids.

I: Ha-ha, but you said you damaged the soles of your sport shoes yesterday! Did you buy new ones already?

My brother: No, but how does it matter?

I: How will you go down and play without those shoes?

My brother: Oh! No, I was talking of playing the Candy Crush Saga!

Of course! I should have known better! He's a 21st century child. Of course I couldn't expect him to play old-fashioned games like seven stones and football! What was I thinking?

Children of the new age rely on technology for a majority of their play, grossly limiting their creativity and imagination, as well as limiting necessary challenges to their bodies to achieve optimal, sensory and motor development. Sedentary bodies bombarded with chaotic sensory stimulation are resulting in delays in attaining child developmental milestones, with subsequent negative impact on basic foundation skills. Hard-wired for high speed, today's young are entering school struggling with self-regulation and attention skills necessRehan for learning, eventually becoming significant problems for teachers in the classroom.

I once asked a 12-year old reader (yeah, those typical old-fashioned children who surprisingly still love to read – not from a Kindle, but from yellowed paper!) the difference between reading a book and watching its movie. She said, "It's the difference between skydiving and watching someone else skydive. When you read, the world is yours to create; you are free to conjure up whatever you feel like. When you watch, you watch. You see someone else's imagination. And for that matter, your imagination might be way higher than theirs, in which case, you're missing out on that!"

No people! I'm not anti-technology. I'm just against anti-overuse of technology. You want an AC? Have it! Just don't forget the wonders of the open meadows. You want a tablet? Use it! Just don't forget the perks of reading a real paper-back book. You want to experience the "good" of the tech-world? Keep out the "bad"! Laugh, learn and live (off the internet too!)!

*   *   *   *

Concentrate on yourself

"You can't found a company if you do not live,"

"Yeah, I see, dead people cannot start a start-up because... let me think... Oh! They're dead!" I try some sarcasm.

"There are too many dead people around us!"

"You mean this place is haunted?"

"Yeah, exactly. For instance, let's take a look at the sample sitting next to me," we turn to look at Prajit, who is busy mutilating the keyboard of his tablet and has no time to look up, "Pieces like this exist all around us. In fact, nowadays our virtual existence seems to carry much more value than our physical existence. What was this latest fad now?"

"The Candy Crush Saga?" I offer.

"No, no, the other one," Shan Sir squints as he tries to recall. I wander aimlessly down memory lane, trying to recollect all the pointless fads that have ever walked the face of Facebook, Instagram and Twitter. From 'Who has a secret crush on you?' (HELL! It's supposed to be 'secret' for a reason!) to 'Who misses you most?' (A few decades ago, Sir Alexander Graham Bell discovered this crazy old machine called the telephone which does this crazy old thing called 'ringing' when somebody who misses you does this crazy old thing called 'trying to contact'); from hash-tags (#I #love #mah #besties #khan't #livewithoutem #best-friend-love #khan't #writeinenglish #khan't #spellanything #didn #attend #kindergarten #failed #playschool #grammar) to commenting "Gurl! U luk smokin' hawt!" on every picture on your news feed - there's barely anything left for a zombie Apocalypse to come true.

"Oh! The ice-bucket challenge?" it strikes me.

"Yeah, that! You know, one upon a time, when research proved that humans existed, there used to be this absolutely stupid concept of donating to the charity anonymously. That means, even the charity didn't know who was making the donations! Can you believe that? I mean, isn't that insane?" Shan Sir feigns surprise, "And now, people are openly posting videos of themselves bathing in ice to prove how 'cool' they are before even considering to make the donation!"

"Sad,""We've become too engrossed in others' affairs. We want to know what others are up to. What is the 'trendiest' topic around? What is the name of your ex-boyfriend's current girlfriend's uncle's grandfather's mother-in-law's servant's dog? Where did your boss's son go for his honeymoon? Mauritius? Oh! That's so mainstream! We can't stop thinking about others all the while. I have noticed that this attitude manifests itself in the business world too! And when that happens, you lose interest in your own endeavours and get too caught up in other people's! That reduces the dedication and passion you had for your dream. And that in turn, ruins everything. And that's the end of it all. Thanks to your virtual social existence, you've successfully wrecked what could have been an opportunity for a lifetime!"

[21]
BE UPFRONT

'I don't have to regret anything!'

There is something ravishingly attractive about honesty and frankness. Because whether you want to believe it or not, people easily find out when you are lying or even layering. And guess why? Because they are human! They know exactly what you want and what you're thinking. In fact, some of them are likely to get hugely annoyed if you try to sweet talk them into ANY-f***ing-thing.

We all have that one friend we fall in love with (irrespective of gender) just because she is irresistibly upfront (and that makes her hawwwwt) Yeah Diya, I'm talking about you, love. And yeah, it's in public. Yeah, you can stop blushing and freaking out. No, don't begin making arrangements for my murder tonight as yet. I'll give you more reasons to begin the planning. Just you wait! You know you love me.

Well, so here's the deal:

It was Valentine's Day, 2014. I was (am) single. Diya was (is) single. She asked me out. Or did I? Anyway, one of us asked the other of us out and the other of us jumped at the idea. This was what the other of us had been waiting for all our lives. And right then, right there, she had the girl of her dreams right in front of her.

(Okay, enough of the cheese already)

So, we arranged a date at Pizza Corner (an on-campus eatery) and went out with bed-crazy hair, pyjamas, and wild red eyes. As expected, as soon as we entered, everyone's attention turned from their dates to us as we strutted in with our severely mentally-wrecked, dishevelled looks. We were 'head-turners' in the most literal sense of the word! I'm not sure but I think I even heard someone say, "They are meant for each other!"

"Dudette, do you think we should have put on some of the gooey, sticky, powdery, painted stuff on our faces? It seems like people are not really very excited about the just-woke-up-and-rushed-for-a-date look," I asked uncomfortably shifting under the glares of the pretty boys and dolled-up girls.

"You mean make-up?"

"Yeah, you know. I think that's what it's called out here,"

"OH COME ON! Sweetheart! I washed my face for you! If that isn't enough, what is?"

Actually, that was more than enough! Getting Diya to wash her face was a challenge not many could conquer. I gave in.

"You know why they're staring at us like that Anamika?" she whispered.

I blinked.

"They're just jealous. They're jealous that we get to love each other even at our worst while they get to see only the painted side of the person they pretend to love!"

Now, tell me who can resist that! Girls, I assure you, there will come a day in your life when you'll regret not marrying your best girlfriend and ending up with a completely different Martian species. But by then, it will already have been too late. I can foresee it. I pity you. I feel you.

Dear future husband,

Your biggest competitor isn't a guy. It'll never be a guy. If I tell you I like you, it means 'I like you amongst all the GUYS I know.' But every time you piss me off, I'll be right by your side, breathing down your neck and reminding you how insignificant you are in front of Diya!

So anyway, halfway into the date, we began to talk about each other to each other (What else? Duh! It's a date, remember?) A lot of time and love later, I asked her what she found to be the most irritating thing about me.

"You sugar-coat things, Anamika!" she replied instantly.

"Give me an example," I demanded giving her my infamous killer-look.

She rolled her eyes, thought for a while and came up with the 'most appropriate example' according to her, "Look, if someday, you go to a rave party, get wasted and end up having sex with a total stranger whose name you forget to ask, you know what you'll tell me the next day? You'll tell me, 'I made love to him!' while knowing fully well that you don't even know his first name! Do you realise what a wrong impression this will give me? I'll think you actually 'fell in love' with the guy! But no! You didn't. You just… you know, did it in the heat of the moment! What you're actually supposed to say is: 'You know Diya, I met this hot guy out at a rave party, got drunk with him and had sex!' And trust me, I would say just that – even if I was telling my Mom about it! Yeah, she would chop my head off, but that's okay. She'd regret it later. I wouldn't have to regret ANYTHING!"

I stared at this girl wide-eyed for the next few minutes. Why the hell was she a girl? She was so right! And she knew me better than I knew myself! Yes, that was the first time I realised that I do sugar coat things a bit – just so that it sounds better to my own self!

"You have a divine idea of me, don't you? Rave parties, getting wasted, one-night stands, too much hotness in one night – what better could I ask for from a valentine?"

The next moment, we were rolling around the place clutching our stomachs and laughing so hard that we managed to ruin the romantic setting all over again! But yeah, there's always a little bit of truth in the wildest of jokes.

*   *   *   *

'But is it safe to tell everything to everyone?'

"How upfront should one be in the real... er, corporate world?" I asked, blatantly.

"Just as upfront as you are now!"

"But then, wouldn't that create a mess out there? If everyone actually started speaking their minds, then I'm sure the world will turn into a living hell!" I said, imagining what might happen if all my thoughts were out in the open for everyone to see. People would have hanged themselves from the nearest tree!

Shan Sir laughed, "Depends on what you call 'hell'. The world will change for sure – but whether into heaven or into hell, I can't say. Personally, I find double-faced people worthy of hell. If you're a bad person, be bad on my face! If you're a good person, don't pretend to be good only to my face!"

"If bad people were bad on your face, they wouldn't be bad at all!" I sighed.

"There, young lady, you get that right! So how can hell exist without bad people?"

"True that,"

"In Fix Nix, everyone knows everything about everything. Right from salaries to technical glitches to financial glitches – you ask them, they'll know it, every single one of my Nixers,"

"But is it safe to tell everything to everyone?" I wonder aloud.

"No, it involves risks, but take this scenario: You're working at an enterprise with a salary of, say, 4 lakhs and you know there is no hierarchy. How shocking would it be to you if you found out from a colleague that someone else in that same enterprise was being paid 7 lakhs? You may not believe this now, Anamika, but shit like this happens in mega-enterprises too! It's better that the management itself remains transparent and clear for others to peer into. Suppose my company is going through a financial crisis, I shouldn't be ashamed to admit it to all the Nixers myself! There's a certain kind of respect that comes with being clear and true to the people who work for you. When you break the news to them yourself, they become way more conscientious. After that, little things like 'turn off the fans when you leave the room' do not need to be put down in written. The Nixers do it on their own, because they know the reason!"

[22]
DON'T TRY TO VALIDATE IRRATIONAL FEARS

The 'what if'

There are times in college when you feel especially over-worked: when all the assignments, projects, exams, quizzes, research, extra-curriculars, hobbies, friends, boyfriends and whatever-the-hell-you-can-think-of seem to be crushing you at the same time. These are tough times, I admit. But hey, just because they are tough times doesn't mean you begin to act in the most crazed fashion you can dream of. Here's a snippet of a conversation I had with Diya last semester:

I: Diya, I just had a black-out on my way back from the washroom.

Diya (panicked): A black-out? You're kidding, right? What sort of a black-out?

I: The one in which you see nothing but black all around.

Diya: Idiot, I know what a black-out means! I want you to tell me exactly what happened.

I: Well… I was walking down the corridor when all of a sudden, I spun out of control. It was real bad. I barely had consciousness

Diya (giving me the -_- look): That's called 'being giddy'.

I: Yeah, but isn't giddiness a symptom of something bigger?

Diya (still giving me the -_- look): Look, you're hyping stuff. You probably just ran around a little too much under the Vellore sun or skipped a few meals.

I: Yes, but...

Diya: Zip it!

I was almost disappointed at Diya's lack of interest – and hurt too! How dare she tell me I was fine when I clearly believed I wasn't? I knew I was suffering from some incurable disease which must have claimed so many lives before. I decided she just didn't care enough for me. But I was relentless. I would find out what was wrong with me. And I'd do it on my own. I didn't even need a doctor. I was too cool for one!

So this is what I did next: I googled 'black-outs'.

Now Google, for some reason, loves to stab people right in the head when the head is at its most vulnerable.

Guess what? It redirected me to a page for 'seizures', from where I was redirected to a page for 'epilepsy' from where I was in turn redirected to a page for 'lack of motor control and psychological delusions', from where I was redirected to a page for 'nervous system damage' from where I was redirected to a page for 'brain tumour', from which I was redirected to a page for 'cancer'.

That's it! I was dying! I had cancer! I had diagnosed myself!

I had to be put on sedatives that night so I wouldn't create more of a scene in the room.

*   *   *   *

"What were your worst fears in the beginning?"

"That's easy: the fear of failure, of course! But that was invalid from the start."

My green monster begins to raise its neck yet again. How the heck can anyone KNOW that they were invalid? I had feared death out of dizziness!

"Yeah, okay, they were invalid. But how did you know?"

Prajit sets off into bouts of laughter, driving me even more green, "Anamika, say you really want to work in a research lab, say Cold Spring Harbor and you'd kill for it. You are ready to do whatever it takes for it. You've written to the scientists asking them the procedure to train under them for at least a little while. They reply saying that you have o fill in an application and they'll judge whether you will be a fit in their lab. What would you do?""I would send in an application,"

"Yes, you would,"

"Yes, I would," I repeat, wondering where this was leading.

"Exactly, yes, you would. But before that you'd have fears like:

- That's the lab James Watson founded! Holy Hell! Why would a Nobel prize winner even care to look at the worthless second year student I am
- Harvard students don't get in. Who am I again?
- It's so far away from India. Mom would hate me if I had to leave. It's not like she's ever been impressed by me anyway
- … And the list goes on

Does that mean you wouldn't even give it a shot? Chances of making it are small. The future is blurred (as a Delhi winter!) but if you keep validating those fears, you've lost even before you've begun to crawl! Live with regret for the rest of your life or fail hard or win - it's your call!"

[23]
SELL WHATEVER YOU HAVE

If nothing, sell your vision!

One fine Sunday morning, a couple of days before the commencement of Anamika's overly hyped "twelfth boards", her darling brother very conveniently decided to throw a tantrum which could have easily qualified as World War III. Apparently, his 'seniors' at the tennis class had asked him which 'brand' of racquet he used. And to his utter embarrassment, he had to draw up a blank face. This was a shame he couldn't tolerate. His world was shattering into bits in front of his own eyes! Everything he had ever achieved made no sense at all. His only achievement now lay in GETTING A

BRANDED RACQUET!

I was amazed beyond limits at human stupidity that day. (It's not like it has ever failed to amaze me. But that day, it was an extraordinary revelation). All these days, I just would sit and stare at all the ten-year old siblings of all my poor friends when they asked for iPhones and iPads just to 'maintain status in society'. (Phew! I sometimes really wonder what will become of our society when these ten-year olds grow up (if they ever do, that is. I've no idea how they'll manage to do that in the first place) and begin to handle the world. When I was 10, my 'society' comprised primarily of Tom, Jerry, unicorns and mermaids. They were so sweet they never even tried to coax me to 'maintain status.' I guess that's the sole reason I always had better things to do.) But when it comes from your own sibling, you stand there aghast – and absolutely convinced you should disown him immediately! I only wish it was as easy as it sounds.

Everyone was immensely mad at him. Mom wouldn't talk to him. Dad had already tried to knock some sense into his impenetrable pea-brain. I had my neurons crossed for him. Since I couldn't disown him (legal issues, you know), I prayed for his soul. "May the Almighty reveal to my little brother that he's being a complete ass. Amen."

But guess what? God decided against that too! He friggin' supported my brother... But honestly, He ended up teaching me tons of things in one sentence.

You see, kids are armed with so many things that adults blatantly lack. The most important of these is 'belief'. Yeah, remember that word that used to be present in those 16th century novels? The word that we think doesn't exist anymore? The word that loses all meaning the first time something breaks our heart? The word that you now laugh off as 'imaginary'?

Folks, I hate to break this to you but you've been getting it wrong all your lives. This word holds wonders. This word fuels a fire you've perhaps never even begun to experience. My brother believed. He BELIEVED he deserved a branded racket (Okay, honestly, on a scale of one to ten, how stupid does that sound?) But he did! He believed in it with an intensity I'd never known before!

This is an excerpt from the conversation that ensued between Rehan and Dad:

Rehan: Dad, please! I'll never ask for anything else in my entire life (Disclaimer: This "entire life" lasted for at most 10 minutes)

Dad (still trying to talk sense): But for once, tell me WHY!

Rehan: Because they're asking me!

Dad: If they ask you to jump into a well tomorrow, will you do that just because they're asking you to? (Yeah, that age-old cliché)

Rehan (hesitates and shakes head in denial): No…

WOW! This line still works, I wondered. I must make a note to use this on my future kids. It's safely stowed away in my cerebrum now.

Dad: Then?

Rehan (with those extremely irritating statement tears in his eyes): But I still want it!

Dad (STILL trying to talk sense): Why?

Rehan (matter-of-factly): I NEED to endorse a brand when I go to Wimbledon, don't I?

That's it!

He'd dropped the bomb.

One sentence had done what three hours hadn't. Dad was speechless. Mom was wide-eyed. I was blown off. This kid here wasn't joking about Wimbledon. The look on his face said that he was a hundred and one per cent serious. But HOW could he be? I knew he was passionate about tennis. I knew he had set goals for himself. I knew he trained extremely hard. But WIMBLEDON? He's 10 for God's sake!

But the trick had been done. He got his 'Head' that day (Head happens to be a popular brand which Djokovic endorses). I must say he was elated with his newfound 'Head'. Now, wherever he went, his 'Head' would tag along.

A day or two later, when I asked Dad why he couldn't just ignore Rehan's rubbish, he replied in just one sentence, "He was genuine; he had a vision,"

*   *   *   *

"A few years ago, I took a short business trip to Mumbai where I met the chief security officer of Cipla at a NASSCOM conference," Shan Sir says.

"Yeah, you have contacts," I admitted.

He laughs, "It's not about contacts. Let me get to the point. As it turns out, we talked for quite a while that day, discussing the problems faced in security and the possible solutions. And obviously, as is the custom, we exchanged business contacts. I'd told him exactly what I intended to make and what purposes it would serve. He asked me if I had any part of it already prepared. But to me, it was just an idea. I was hopeful it would take tangible shape soon, but for that time period, it was just a vision statement. We crossed paths and then, went our respective ways. A year and a half later, I discovered that Cipla was facing the same issues that we'd been working on so far. One call to the chief security officer and I scheduled a 15-minute appointment just before the lunch break. The call went something like this:

I: Sir, this is Shan from FixNix, Inc.. We met at the Mumbai NASSCOM conference if you remember?

He: Oh, yes! FixNix, Inc.!

I: I have something important to tell you Sir, if you could kindly make some time. I'm sure it would benefit us.

He: But I have a packed schedule right now, Sir.

I: That's fine, even 15 minutes would be enough!

He: I wouldn't really have entertained more guests, but since it's you, I wouldn't dare deny.

I was so glad I had reached out to him before. Now that we had the solution ready, I knew he would like it,"

"So you sold him the product in 15 minutes?" I asked bewildered. I do not even have the energy to hit the snooze button in my alarm clock within 15 minutes!

"No, the 15 minutes stretched into a few hours, thanks to his interest. But that day, we had a deal!"

[24]
XENOTHINK: DON'T BE AFRAID TO EXPERIMENT

Losing our sanity

"I can clearly see the future," I announced gravely, "We're going to be the laughing stocks of the entire class, get a thrashing from the teacher and receive negative marks for our assignment! I should consider myself lucky if I got an F grade,"

"You can see nothing like that!" Diya threw me the dirtiest look she could muster, "It's going to be real fun and it will even stretch us to our limits! We'll ourselves know how well (or how gruesome) we are at dramatics and who knows, if Lady Luck smiles down upon us, perhaps someday, you and I will even make it to

Broadway!"

"GOD save me! I'm DONE! So this is what it's all about? Broadway dreams?!"

Our 'Fundamentals of Behavioural Science' teacher had graced us with a project over a month ago. We had had all the time in the world to prepare a proper presentation, all with pretty pictures and stuff. We had had all the time in the world to think of a suitable topic and read and research extensively on it. We had had all the time in the world to even visit a lab related to psychology and neuro-genetics. But lo! Here we were, with eyes full of fear and stress, sitting on our respective beds in our room, one day before the presentation was due and clueless as to how, where and when we should present what. (To all my readers who need classes on procrastination: You're most welcome to our room anytime of the day. We'll never find time for you anyway.)

In times like these (better known as 'crisis situations'), we become so desperate that we begin to cling onto any idea for any project we find (better known as 'a ray of hope'). So Diya had worked up her smart-ass brain and come up with the proposal of presenting a short skit on 'mental disorders and societal reactions to the mentally challenged' and her idea was to portray ME and herself as the 'mentally challenged', while Tamanna would play 'society' and Naina would be the 'therapist'. I revolted at the plan. No other group I knew would have the guts to present a play anyway. Everyone in the world knows PowerPoint presentations are safer any day! On top of that, I was supposed to play the role of a bipolar psyche! What the hell! Why couldn't we simply follow the herd and make another presentation overnight, infuse ourselves with caffeine and go present it to the class the next morning?

"Anamika! Let's try something new for once, please?" Naina intruded.

"You stay out of this. You have a sane role!"

"But seriously Anamika, we KNOW what the other groups are planning on doing – the same clichéd presentations! Why can't we be different for once?"

"We'll end up with nothing, I'm warning you... And Diya, trash your Broadway dreams. It's about time,"

"Hey pessimist!" Tamanna quipped, "We'll end up with nothing. Or, we'll end up with everything. At least, we won't be ordinRehan,"

I reflected, "How high are the stakes?"

"50-50,"

"There'll be a price to pay if we don't make it big, you know that right?"

The other three nodded in unison.

I gave up with a sigh, "Okay then, game on!"

That was by far one of the most memorable nights I've ever had in my life. They couldn't stop laughing trying out different outfits, different hairstyles, different postures, different eye movements, spooky gestures, crazy (in the most literal sense of the word), schizophrenic and bipolar expressions... Oh! And a hell lot of selfies, which, if released to the public, would create unrest, havoc and reinstate belief of the masses in the theories of spirit-invasions.

The next day, when we had to finally present it in the class, we got caught up in nerves. What if nothing worked out? What if everything turned out to be a failure? What if... (a zillion other questions)

Once on stage, nothing else mattered. We forgot about the audience; we forgot about the light; we forgot about the classes; we forgot about the teacher – all we could remember was the epic fun we'd had the previous night. We did justice to all the body language, facial and hand gestures and eye-rolling we'd learnt a few hours before. We did justice to the night. Most importantly, we did justice to the coffee that had flooded our systems.

I don't remember how I acted. I don't remember if Diya got any call from a Broadway director that evening. I don't remember if we scored a 10 on 10 or a 0 on 10 for the assignment. All I remember was the standing ovation we received from our classmates and the beaming face of our teacher as she congratulated us after the performance. We were elated at the response and celebrating like crazy (figuratively) when the teacher approached us from behind, took me and Diya aside and whispered to us, "You two were the best fits for the roles you chose!"

I'm still trying to figure out if that was a compliment or an insult.

"See Anamika, there's at least something we're good at!"

"Yeah, you know why Diya?"

"Why?"

"Because we didn't even have to act onstage. We were our normal selves you see!"

Diya burst out laughing, "I'm so glad we had the guts to think out of the box though,"

"SEE! That's because we're ACTUALLY cracked in the head!"

"That's a little derogatory to the mentally ill!"

"Not when the mentally ill say it for their own selves though!"

*   *   *   *

"When you know that the stakes are high, you tend to play it safe. That has to be ditched! I've gained so much from playing with fire,"

"What sort of gains?"

"Well, when I first embarked on this journey, I was told to go for more 'experienced' people who have thrived in the corporate world (in short, the oldies) because they would know exactly how things work,"

"You refused," I'd got to know Shan Sir so well now. He could hardly surprise me anymore. I was immune.

"Exactly, I refused. I created my own young, rugged team of rookies who would never pass the buck for 'experience'! But then, each one of them brought something new to the table. Because they weren't already conditioned to thinking on the trodden lines, they thought on a variety of different lines. Result: We got a number of solutions to a proposed problem, out of which we could filter out a combination of the best and the most novel. It has always done me good to have a young team with me. They work, not just for the heck of it. They work because they enjoy learning! My experiments with them have never been futile. Also, it does no harm to ask the youth exactly what it needs!"

[25]
EMBRACE YOURSELF

'Some people are just not supposed to be sweet!'

By now, I guess you've got accustomed to this character called Diya in my life, who happens to be the biggest troll I have ever set my optic nerve on. I love to think I know an immense lot about her. But every time I think I have her all figured out and nothing about her can surprise me anymore, there tags along another incident which makes me completely forget who she is, throws her picture into the nearest pit I find, and makes me question the meaning and purpose of her life... It's sad, you know, very sad. (Diya, I have tears of your pain in my eyes, see? (!_!)

Anyway, so getting along with the story, this is what happened a week after the 13th of August:

One of our ex-roommates had had her birthday on the 13th. A week later, it suddenly struck us that we should have got her a present at least, however small.

"Dudette, do you think it's too late now?" Diya asked, contemplative.

"It's one week past her birthday. She must have forgotten it herself by now!" I agree.

Diya gave me the "what-the-heck-are –you-talking-about" look, "Do you remember your birthday, Anamika? It was so far back sometime in March, right? You must have forgotten it, right?"

"Hey, I don't remember who gave me what present at least!" I retorted.

Apparently, that wasn't the best thing to say at that time, probably because my friends had arranged a surprise party for me right in the middle of the night (Gifts included). So that's how I managed to piss Diya off that evening.

One thing of interest about this girl is: Whenever she is pissed off for some reason or another, she suddenly becomes inexplicably sweet to everyone around her. (Yeah, most of the time, she is a mean bitch. Sorry Diya, but I don't think that's a secret anymore. But well, that's who she is! That's what makes Diya "Diya". And everyone around her loves her that way! So if she begins to get sweet, it makes us extremely uncomfortable. And she knows it and uses it to the best of her advantage. How sweet, right?)

So that evening, we went to All Mart, bought the necessary gifts for our ex-roommate and were on our way back to the hostel. As luck would have it, on the way, we met a senior who Diya knew, but didn't really like too much. What happened next was hilarious! In her "pissed-off-oh-so-sweet" mood, Diya stopped near the walkway to talk to him. He informed her that he'd been placed at Hike. Under usual circumstances, the "true" Diya would have just congratulated him pleasantly and moved on. But this was the 'still-angry' Diya. So this is the conversation that followed:

Senior: Yeah, and by the way, I just got placed at Hike!

Diya: Oh, that's terrific... Yeah, I mean that's so awesome! I'm so happy for you, bhaiyya! I can't believe it! So, where's the party? I can't wait for the treat!

Me (to Anamika): Dude! She sounds drunk! Have you ever seen her talk that way to anyone ever?

Anamika (to me): She's cold out, man. God save her and the world.

Senior: Of course, tell me where you'd like to go. Let's go sometime!

Diya (suddenly returning to her senses in a jolt): What?

You're actually willing to give me a treat?

Senior: Of course! You just tell me if you're free next weekend. Leave the rest onto me.

Diya: Oh, I'm sorry but we have exams next week.

Me (to Anamika): LOL! She's suggesting that she has to study??? No better escape route, eh?

Senior: Then next to next week, perhaps?

Diya: Oh, I think I'd be busy with Gravitas then...

Senior: That's a packed-up schedule.

Diya: I'm afraid so. I'm all packed-up this semester, you see?

Senior: Okay, we'll see about the treat then...

Diya: You know what? Forget it! I'm happy for you – that's it. I don't need you to treat me to prove that you're happy too.

Senior (disappointed): Oh, well...

End of conversation

The moment we take a turn and begin to walk back, I burst!

"WHAT was THAT?" I asked, crying tears of laughter.

"DUDE!!! I barely know that guy! How am I supposed to

go out for a 'treat' with him?" she howled.

"And what were you doing BEFORE that fact struck you?"

"Well, you know, I was just... I was just trying to be sweet to him for once! I didn't know I'd get myself into such hot soup by being nice!"

"You know what, Diya! Quit being nice... Because whenever you've tied to be nice, you've had to swim out of some really sticky situation! I know this is hard for you to digest, but you know some people are just not supposed to be sweet! They're supposed to be... You know, MEAN! They're supposed to be... Themselves!"

Diya nodded solemnly in agreement for a while. Then, the confession struck, "Wait a minute! You just said I'm mean!"

Anamika shook her head innocently, "I never SAID it; I just implied it!"

Well, that night, I lay in bed nursing bruised arms and watching tweeties swirling around my head. But oh, well... At least I'd saved Diya from being 'sweet' anymore! And someday, she's going to thank me for this. (I'm still patiently waiting for the day that she ever utters the magic words 'Thank you' from her mouth, but it's said we should never lose hope, so...

*   *   *   *

'That's just the way I roll!'

"I remember there was this one time when we'd had to leave for Kenya for a conference and some work. We were supposed to go as a group and everything was just fine before we reached the hotel,"

"What was wrong at the hotel?"

"You see, I'm hardly interested in 5-star plazas when I'm abroad for travel. All the 5-star and 7-star resorts look exactly the same inside out everywhere on the planet. So what difference does it make if I'm in Kenya or in India if I'm supposed to live in a 5-star palace? You get to know absolutely nothing about the place and its people. It's not worth the visit! So I ditched the 5-star accommodation and set off on my own to look for a smaller and more Kenya-ish cottage to live in, and in the process, I guess I made some of my group members mad at me,"

"You guess?"

"Well, now that you ask me, no, not just guess. I was sure. Half-way out of the suite, one of them literally asked me on the face if I was a little slow in the head."

"You've had people asking you if you were a retard?!" I laugh aloud. Oh, how Diya would love that!

"Yes, precisely that,"

"What did you reply then?"

"Oh you can guess. I pretended nodded like a retard and said, 'Dude, that's just the way I roll' and left the place immediately,"

"Poor guy! You could have stayed, couldn't you? For courtesy's sake?"

"You mean as a social obligation?"

"Yeah, yeah, I know that sucks, but..."

"No, Anamika! I have a phobia of social obligations!"

I laugh, "I can relate!"

"I believe you need to be true to who you are at every point in your life. No matter how small or big the decision is, you need to make sure it's YOU who's making the decision and not the society! If you want to eat a vanilla ice-cream instead of chocolate, eat vanilla! Don't care if they think it's against the 'rules'. Who the hell authors all the rule-books of the world anyway?"

[26]
ZAP OUT OF THE FEAR OF INFLUENCE!

'Because you alone are enough.'

December 24, 2013: Two years had passed since I had last seen her – two years of incessant prayers, two years of incessant tears. Finally, everything seemed to have paid off. Finally, everything seemed to be returning to normal again. Finally, we saw it for what it was – a great, long nightmare. Finally, she'd returned to the weird old world with a fresh new perspective. Finally, she had won the battle against a disease so dreadful it wreaks havoc in not just the patient, but in all the people who care. Finally, she had won the battle against cancer.

December 24, 2013: There was such a huge crowd at the

entrance of her ward that I considered it better to wait outside until the crowd subsided a little. Morning turned into afternoon, afternoon flowed into evening, evening shifted to dusk – and ultimately, at 7.30 pm, I had the privilege to meet the 'classmate' who had metamorphosed into 'one of my best friends' fifteen years ago. She had changed now. Of course, she had. But that was expected. Chemo had visibly taken its toll on her body. I just hoped her mind had remained unscathed. The moment I entered, she turned to me and smiled.

I knew that very instant that something was amiss. That smile – she used to have the sort of smile that could convey volumes; she used to have the sort of smile that could heal all brokenness; she used to have the kind of smile that would not just reach her eyes, but would penetrate into others'. You know such smiles when you see them – the contagious sort of smiles. Not just giggle and teeth, but true, tangible happiness. Today, I realised that was amiss. Today, she was just giggle and teeth. Today, she was not smiling. Today, she was acting. And even though she made a fabulous actress in our school plays, she couldn't deceive her best friends through drama.

I waited till the façade had to be maintained. I waited till the other guests had left the ward. I waited till she had socialised enough. I waited till I was alone in the room with her. She sensed it. As soon as we were left to ourselves, she picked up the nearest book she could find and began to flip through the pages, thinking she could deceive me.

"Hey Rhea! Long time! How've you been?" I tried to begin with some small-talk.

"Yeah, fantastic! I'm so glad it's all over though!" she laughed, not raising her eyes from her book. I was amused. She knew her weaknesses. She could never look a person in the eye and lie. She had to look away when she was lying. It was absolutely necessRehan for her. This inexplicable issue of hers had gotten us into trouble several times in school. Whenever we bunked a class to go to the school café, we HAD to go to the librRehan once too! Because otherwise, one look at Rhea's eyes, and all the teachers could tell that the innocent "We've been to the library," was a big fat lie!

I decided I had had enough, "Rhea, stop it! Tell me what's wrong,"

Rhea knew I'd get to her sooner or later. So, she wasn't half surprised at my outburst. "Have you ever been petrified, Anamika?" she raised her eyes from the book she'd been pretending to read all along, "Not scared, not even frightened, but absolutely, mind-numbingly petrified?"

I was taken aback. This wasn't exactly what I'd expected. The Rhea I used to know was brave, strong, independent and carefree. The Rhea I used to know would take on anything in the world and stop nowhere. The Rhea I used to know would never settle for anything less than what she knew she deserved. The Rhea I used to know would strive to death and yet, never be scared of anyone on the planet.

*   *   *   *

Once, when I was especially nervous before an Indo-jazz performance in an inter-state dance competition, I had called her up. She had been the only one I knew who I could approach for the best possible pep-talk.

"What if I mess up? You know how much this means to the team. I can't be a moron and let them down! They don't need me to win this. I'm just going to create a ruckus onstage. I think I should just quit. One member would make no difference in a group of 10."

She was silent for a while, "I'm amazed at what an utter fool you can be, Anamika! I never thought you'd turn out to be this stupid. You've fooled yourself into thinking that you're being 'oh-so-selfless' and 'paving way for the greater good' by running away, but you can't fool me! I'm better than that! What you're doing is so blatantly selfish that I'm almost reluctant to call you my friend anymore. You want to quit the group and shatter their faith in you at the eleventh hour? You want to desert them at the very last minute after all the belief they had in you? You want to be nothing more than a traitor after all the resources, money and time they've spent in grooming you into the beautiful dancer you are today? Is that what you want? You want to prove to them that they were wrong in investing their trust on you? If that's what you want, go ahead, quit! I can't stop you. I can just pity you... But as a friend, I'd request you to reconsider,"

"And what if one of them messes up? What if everyone else ruins the performance? What do I do then? All MY efforts would go straight to the trash!"

That was the first time she'd revealed her secret mantra, "One thing you need to know Anamika, is that you alone are enough. You stay strong, do your bit; don't even care about the others – because you know what? You alone are enough. You are so enough that my words aren't enough to tell you how enough you are. Always remember that, Anamika. Always,"

We aced the performance that night.

*   *   *   *

What had murdered the Rhea I used to know? What had happened to the Rhea whose heart was free and whose spirit, indomitable? Had she ultimately succumbed to cancer? Had I lost the Rhea who I used to know?

I shook my head in denial, pulled her closer and said, "No, I don't think I have ever been petrified, Rhea. And neither should you be. What's wrong?"

"What is wrong is that I am. I am petrified, Anamika! I can't take it anymore. I am petrified," that was the first day in fifteen years that I saw her eyes glazed. But she held back the tears – like she always had.

"Rhea! Buckle up, girl! You're a strong young lady!"

Rhea smiled a smile so unnatural it did not even reach her eyes, "Strength is a strong word, Anamika. Yes, I am strong because all these days, I didn't let the terror get to me. Yes, I am strong because all these days you've never seen me shed a single tear. Yes, I am strong because I camouflage my heart so well that the scars are barely visible to me! But this isn't a scar, Anamika. This is sheer, raw terror. This is a wound that hasn't stopped bleeding since I was diagnosed. Strength is relative, Anamika. Somewhere deep inside, I think all of us are equally vulnerable. Some cry oceans to let it all out, others become vacant – vacant words, vacant eyes, vacant expressions, vacant minds. There are words in their throats, lumps of accumulated silences. You can't always call the emptiness 'strength',"

I marvelled at the way she thought. I marvelled at the depth of her being. But most of all, I marvelled at the person she was, "Tell me your terrors, Rhea. Perhaps, we can chase them away – together,"

Rhea smiled again, distantly, "I'm petrified of happiness,

Anamika. It makes me numb with fear. Tell me how you can help me,"

I was at a loss of words. I have always considered myself to be a keen listener. So, these ears of mine have heard quite a lot of astonishing things – but this surpassed them all. Even the most neurotic people I had heard of did not have 'cherophobia'. It was just a term with no real significance to me. And now, all of a sudden, it had jumped off the psychology textbooks and into the brain of my invincible friend!

"Why? Why does it petrify you, Rhea? Don't you DESERVE to be happy? Isn't happiness the reason of our existence? You NEED to be happy!"

"Exactly, Anamika! I'm scared of 'needing' anything – including happiness! Because as soon as I begin to 'need' something, I lose it! This happens essentially every single time! I thought I needed journalism. I found it for a little while. Then, I lost it. I had to drop out of a course I had yearned for my entire life! I thought I needed you. You left the city. I thought I needed a healthy physique. They diagnosed me at the pre-final stage of a disease which apparently has no cure. Now, I think I need happiness. And I'm so sure I'm going to lose it that it hurts to even need it! I even lost all my hair, Anamika! I used to be so fond of it!" she fixes me with a momentary glint of humour in on her faded face. "I don't know if I'm making sense to you, but after everything that happened,

I'm petrified... of hope and happiness!"

No amount of logic could make her see how irrational she sounded. She didn't care. To her, it didn't matter anymore. She had given up on the only two things that made life worthwhile. She didn't see a reason to live anymore. She just survived. It was unimaginably difficult to break her. But when she broke, she'd broken hard! She'd broken her own self!

That moment, I decided to do something so crazy that I don't think I can ever forget it. I got up from the couch, walked straight to the washroom mirror, took a pair of scissors and a razor and shaved off all my hair. I took a tissue paper from the roll, got a toothpick and wrote (tore), "I am here. You have me back"

Then, I waltzed back to her bed and said, "You haven't lost me. I am here," and gifted the tissue, "And of course you loved your hair. I loved mine too! I still do. The only difference: I hope and believe that mine will grow back in a couple of months. That makes it so much easier to laugh at my reflection in the mirror today because I don't just hope; I BELIEVE it will all come back tomorrow and I'll have to take the pains to tie it all up again. So, today, why not feel light-headed and merry! We have our whole lives to stay with the same length of hair! If today, we can experience something new, why not experience it with pleasure! Because Rhea, when tomorrow, everything returns back to normal, we'll regret not enjoying today; we'll regret not living differently. Not many people get to choose to be different. If life has blessed you with the opportunity, go grab it! Whine and you won't even notice it! And honestly, regret sucks!"

I spent the next few weeks roaming the city with her in my brand new avatar! We ran barefoot on the dewy meadows, we skipped snacks to watch sunsets, we cooked up brilliant disasters in the kitchen, we got ourselves into truckloads of trouble, we wrote each other love letters (which we later even posted anonymously to no one in particular), we melted chocolate in pressure cookers and baked cookies out of them, we cut flowers from the garden, we spent the nights on our rooftops gazing at the stars and arguing which direction Peter Pan would come from and how angry Tinker Bell would be if Peter took one of us on a date, we ate sixteen tubs of gourmet in one night, we suntanned ourselves (till we were almost invisible in darkness), we got high on caffeine and sunrises, we dressed ourselves up as bald fairy princesses and strutted around the neighbourhood in tiaras made of grass, we made a royal canopy and coronet for our beds from old school uniforms, we wore suspender belts with stockings just for the heck of it, we wrote to the President of India about what we would like to call the 'National Food', we went to a real estate agent and made her show us houses way above our 'affordable range' (Our 'affordable range' was a Barbie house), pretended to seriously consider them and called our parents to check if they were fine with it... Most importantly, we breathed life into our lives. We, for once, truly lived!

A month later, I had to leave the city again. I had to return to college; I had to return to routine. The last night, as we were having our final quota of cappuccino, I'd tried to insinuate how much I was going to miss her, "This place has some of my happiest memories. I'm really going to miss this place,"

But Rhea was no novice to subtlety. When she replied, I almost heard a taunt in her voice, "Yeah, 'this place' is going to miss you a lot too,"

I loved that tease. She knew what I was thinking – and we both sat there under the starry sky, comfortable in our own silences, drinking every word from each other's minds. They say you can find meaning in someone else's quietude only if you care too much. We both cared too much. We both knew it.

"You're happy, Rhea, aren't you?" that was the first time I'd ever brought up the topic again.

"I am. I'm elated. I'm wondrously happy. And you know you are the one who made me," she threw me a side glance. I saw the smile return. The Rhea I once knew had returned from the grave. No one and nothing could break her spirit ever again. Cancer was just another zodiac sign. Everything was perfect. Her world was as calm as the early waves.

"But I'm slightly worried. Not the neurotic stuff I told you earlier this month – just a little disturbed," she continued.

"Why?"

"What if I am happy but others don't let me? What if someone I love messes up? What if someone I care about ruins everything? What do I do then? All my efforts to stay happy would go straight to the trash!"

I smiled; I knew this feeling so well it stung! "One thing you need to know Rhea, is that you alone are enough. You stay strong, do your bit; don't even care about the others – because you know what? You alone are enough. You are so enough that my words aren't enough to tell you how enough you are. Always remember that, Rhea. Always."

*   *   *   *

'He just got lucky the first time.'

"What is the lowest you've felt throughout this journey?" I ask. It's my final question and I intend to pack up after this.

"Whenever I've heard people talk," comes the reply.

"I know. People talk."

At the end of the summer semester of 2012, Prajit met with an accident, leaving both his legs badly injured.

"That was a depressive phase to say the least," he reflects.

After a year of rigorous efforts, everything seemed to be disappearing into thin air. For over 2 to 3 months, the projects stagnated, the events stalled. There was nothing that was being taken up by the Spartans anymore.

"People get too dependent on one person, you see. And when I lost the power to act efficiently, it all began to crumble apart. There's a sort of terror in it, Anamika - in watching something you've made with so much care and faith, fall apart bit by bit, brick by brick, until even the foundations cease to exist anymore," the way he put it made me shudder.

"And then, obviously, the mockers and haters come around and throw dirt on your face. Those comments still sting when I think about them,"

"What comments?"

"Oh, the ones like 'Look at where he's heading now!', 'I pity his high hopes,' and most of all I felt physical palpable pain when someone I knew told me I'd just got lucky the first time and that I couldn't always rely on luck to make things happen every time. Dammit! That was a burn alright. How does it feel when you go out to the market, buy all the friggin' ingredients for a friggin' cake, come friggin' home, set the friggin' microwave to the friggin' optimum temperature, bake the friggin' cake, melt the friggin' chocolate, garnish it till it's worthy of walking a friggin'... Victoria's secret ramp and then, some random passer-by looks at it and tells you that you didn't even have to bake the cake in the first place because, you know what, apparently 'Fate was super kind to you and made the cake happen Himself!'?"

"I'd have smiled, agreed, punched them in the gut and walked away. And if they dared to call out for help, I'd be like, 'Dude! Just ask Fate, will you? I don't have time... And anyway, helping you will take a lot of hard work, and hard work is too mainstream, right? Toodles!'"

EPILOGUE

"Are you kidding me? You of all people wrote a book? Of course, and oh! Did I mention? I flew to Mars and back!" El has grown up ('aged', she likes to call it) by a few years now.

"It's not funny, El!" I retort, "I'm serious!"

"Supposing, in some obscure surreal setting, I suddenly lost my mind and magically began to believe in all the shit you're giving me. And hypothetically, in some parallel universe, let's also add that you aren't trying hard to impress me," she stifles a giggle, "then, would Your Majesty please tell me what you wrote your book on?" "It's on entrepreneurship," I state boldly.El blinks, "What the heck? You almost sound serious!"

I'm offended. "I AM!" I smart. The next sixty seconds, I revel in the glory of El's surprised silence. For once, I've made her believe me and I know I deserve kudos for that! It's a Herculean task to make El believe in the fact that I'm worth something after all.

The silence soon begins to get to me and I begin to think, "And life too…" I add, after some pondering.

"You've written on entrepreneurship and life?" El's smirk begins to return, "How can you write on both these things at the same time! They're so different from each other!"

"How different?" I challenge.

"Look..." I can see El is struggling to explain, "Entrepreneurship is a hard-core practical real-life thing..." she pauses.

"So you're saying that 'life' is a hard-core impractical unreal-life thing?" I laugh. El is unsure.

"See El, so many things you need to know about entrepreneurship are the same as the ones you need to know about life! It's was Shan Sir called 'tough living'. You need to believe in the best and be prepared for the worst. You need to have an amazing behaviour yourself, but be prepared for the morons who take you for granted. You need to be a nice person and yet be prepared to welcome bad people! The book is just a guide to groom you into your best possible self. Others will falter. Haters will hate. But you be you. That's the crux – both in the business world and in the personal world!"

El looks at me as if I've just metamorphosed into some Greek goddess. I almost blush, "Oh stop you!"

"Di, it's not just me who's a grown-up now," El's eyes almost pop out of their sockets, "You've grown up too!" "Aged, you mean?" I laugh.

"YEAH, SORRY – 'AGED'!"

www.ingramcontent.com/pod-product-compliance
Lightning Source LLC
Chambersburg PA
CBHW020907180526
45163CB00007B/2654